Part I

Behavioral and Social Science Research: A National Resource

Robert McC. Adams, Neil J. Smelser,
and Donald J. Treiman, editors

Committee on Basic Research in the
Behavioral and Social Sciences

Commission on Behavioral and Social Sciences
and Education

National Research Council

NATIONAL ACADEMY PRESS
Washington, D.C.   1982

Library of Congress Catalog Card Number 82-81776

International Standard Book Number 0-309-03278-4

Available from:

NATIONAL ACADEMY PRESS
2101 Constitution Ave., N.W.
Washington, D.C. 20418

Printed in the United States of America

Preface

The Committee on Basic Research in the Behavioral and Social Sciences was established early in 1980 under the auspices of the Assembly of Behavioral and Social Sciences, now the Commission on Behavioral and Social Sciences and Education, of the National Research Council. At the request of the National Science Foundation, the committee was asked to assess the value, significance, and social utility of basic research in the behavioral and social sciences.

One consideration in selecting committee members was to convene a group sufficiently well informed about the huge range of subject matter to oversee a comprehensive study of it. At the same time, however, its size needed to be held within moderate limits in order to deal efficiently with the task at hand. This precluded the appointment of representatives of more than a fraction of the full array of relevant disciplines and subdisciplines.

A second consideration in selecting members was to ensure that they would take a broad, contextual view of the committee's assignment, assessing the progress and potential of the fields within its purview, not exclusively as specialized contributors to them, but with due regard for the interests and concerns of the society at large. For this purpose a number of committee members were chosen whose backgrounds were in other fields of science, in the humanities, and in public life. (Biographical sketches of committee members and staff appear in Appendix B.)

The committee members worked together productively and harmoniously without regard for this diversity, and probably to some extent even because of it. Vigorous differences of opinion arose repeatedly as drafts of the various chapters were prepared, criticized, and repeatedly rewritten, but permanently polarized positions on issues were conspicuous by their absence.

Behavioral and social scientists have sometimes received, and on occasion may even have helped to generate, a variety of criticisms—e.g., that they are overly committed to ideological positions or (somewhat contradictorily) that they are engaged in documenting the trivial and the obvious. Deciding that no abstract refutation of charges at this level of generality is useful or perhaps even possible, in this report the committee has taken little direct cognizance of them. Instead we believe that the report, along with the more detailed papers that accompany it, documents the existence of broad and representative areas of research in these fields, to which such criticisms cannot reasonably be applied.

Some of our illustrative examples of basic research and its products have had the more or less unintended effect of reinforcing the case for particular policies and programs, occasionally on a counterintuitive basis. Others have led to the introduction of new and useful technologies of broad application in the private and public sectors or have altered perceptions of the circumstances with which we cope individually and collectively. And many of them have had the potential of enhancing the well-being of our society and its members. It is partly on a demonstration of these pervasive effects that the case for the social utility of basic research in the behavioral and social sciences rests.

In another sense the committee takes the position that there are dangers in singling out the behavioral and social sciences for measurement against a standard of social utility. Efforts to extend the frontiers of knowledge are fully justifiable in their own terms, dependent only on their progress in altering the scientific understandings that were their original points of departure. In addition, the lack of clear-cut or permanent boundaries around the behavioral and social sciences means that they can be isolated only somewhat arbitrarily and are better understood as part of a wider continuum of scientific and scholarly pursuits. This point was persuasively put by committee member Philip Morrison, a physicist, in a contribution to an early draft of the report. His distinctive breadth of view and vividness of phrase deserve to be recorded:

The very enterprise of a scientific description of the natural world leads directly to the necessity of the social and behavioral sciences. At the eyepiece of the telescope there is a human eye; on the layered strata of the riverbank may be found the flint tools and hearths of prehistoric campsites; the society of bees both forces and gains from a reflective look at the very different society of the entomologist. It does not seem possible to draw any clear line between the scientist looking out at the physical or biological world and another kind of scientist concentrating instead on his or her own species.

As research proceeds it has become ever clearer that the functioning of the eye in terms of its human significance has only a few elementary principles in common with the functioning of a camera. It is instead a complex input device to a computing system more intimately connected to its past than anything constructed in a laboratory. Regularities are discovered in the distribution and cultural composition of ancient campsites, but once again different from those of the coexisting plant and animal communities or of the river deposits that in time covered them. Similarly, it has become clearer and clearer that rules of behavior enforced among bees by transfer of pheromones are secured among humans by a much richer flow of meanings and symbols—grammar, eye contact, flag. This implies simply that the natural sciences must be extended in the same spirit, across what a physical scientist would describe as a phase change, to the study of the extraordinary qualities of the species *Homo sapiens* and its richly diverse works.

Much of what is found in this report elaborates on the nature of the more self-revealing sciences that *H. sapiens* requires. Physical and biological scientists may be disconcerted by the degree to which answers to research questions in the behavioral and social sciences have continually led to the redirection of the questions themselves as well as by the need, when dealing with *H. sapiens*, to devise indirect routes of explanation to replace experiments. But different from the physical and biological sciences though they are, these latter fields share the common goals of all sciences, obey its precepts, and promise its twin fruits, understanding and a measure of choice and control. There is no logical, justifiable cut to make which could part the study of human social and behavioral questions from the traditional and nowadays obligate task of understanding the nonhuman features of the man-made as well as natural world. There may be reason to vary the emphasis, limiting resources in one area while applying them more liberally in another, but the existence of a fundamental continuity cannot be denied. Both the dancer and the dance are proper subjects for the inquiries of science.

At the other end of the spectrum of inquiry and scholarship lie the humanities, with history somehow bridging the intersection. A divergence from the approach common to the sciences may be most evident in the strongly personal nature of many humanistic forms and methods; yet others approximate the techniques and interests of science and hence merge smoothly into the social sciences. Disciplines like anthropology, economics, and political science are becoming familiar terrain for many historians, and the systematizing student of comparative literature (or even the outward-turning novelist) can join forces with sociologists. The linguist or philosopher may find a zone of vital connection still further along the continuum by coming close to mathematics. Once again, in other words, there is no sharp line of division but a broad band of overlapping, common interests. From the specialist in radioactive dating or the biochemist concerned with retinal pigments to the poetic translator of a Babylonian myth sequence, there stretch the hundred specialties of the subjects here under examination. That we confront a complex natural continuum, not a set of differently constituted outlooks that can be linked only by analogy, is perhaps the most essential premise of this or any other close look at the work of a substantial segment of the scientific community today.

At the outset of its work, the committee recognized the need to supplement its own efforts with those of a larger group of colleagues. A small group meeting only a half-dozen times over a period of less than two years could not hope to achieve a balanced and comprehensive assessment if it relied only on its own resources. The most tangible outcome of our attempt to meet this need is the set of commissioned papers that make up Part II of this report, each of them describing in considerable detail a specific area of research and its utilization (see Appendix A for the contents of Part II). A fuller account of how the help of the wider behavioral and social science community was solicited, as well as of how these particular papers were decided upon, may be of interest.

As an initial step, letters outlining the task with which the committee was charged were sent to several hundred leading behavioral and social scientists. These letters acknowledged at the outset a shared commitment to the advancement of basic knowledge as a valid and autonomous goal, but went on to state the need to address questions of priority, utility, and relevance directly and responsibly by those who call on public support as well as by those who allocate it. We suggested that something might be gained by depicting the multiple and diffuse pathways from basic research developments, through assorted channels of application and communication, to tangible public benefit. Flows in the opposite direction, e.g., from applied research findings back to the enrichment of basic scientific understanding, could also be worthy of illustration. More generally, however, we also solicited comment on all aspects of the committee's task. The large number of thoughtful replies received had a profound though necessarily diffuse impact on the direction as well as the specific content of the report.

The committee also recognized the advantage of commissioning a set of special studies reviewing particular research problems or fields, inasmuch as we were asked not only to identify research areas of high social utility but also to review their present and potential contributions. Our letters therefore referred to these plans for commissioned studies and especially invited suggestions of suitable authors, areas, and problems. We received a very large number of concrete and helpful suggestions in response. These were considered in detail by the committee in its early sessions and led to intensive efforts to arrange suitable pairings of authors and subjects.

The studies finally commissioned had in most cases been suggested initially by one or more of the many replies we received. But virtually every subject first went through a process of redefinition by the committee, furthered by discussions with the authors who ultimately undertook the studies. Three of the papers were commissioned jointly with the Social Science Research Council (SSRC), which had been asked by the National Science Foundation to select and oversee the production of a group of papers for the five-year outlook report. Because of the timing of the two projects, SSRC assumed primary responsibility for these papers. More than a third of the committee's meeting time was devoted to the design, selection, and discussion of the entire series of study papers, and the committee is pleased to publish them in conjunction with this report.

Numerous references to the papers appear in the report, mainly to illustrate or amplify specific themes and statements. But my review of their origins and treatment is meant to emphasize that the influence of the papers on the committee's thinking was much more pervasive than these citations suggest. We expect that they will be individually useful and informative to interested nonspecialists, and we also believe that in the aggregate they strongly sustain the committee's case for the diversity, vitality, and utility of the behavioral and social sciences.

It is also a pleasure to acknowledge the efforts of many individuals who have contributed directly to the preparation of the report and the papers. Ernestine Friedl, although not a member of the committee, maintained a special interest in its work as a member of the National Science Board who is also an anthropologist. In this capacity she met and functioned with the committee throughout the study, contributing to the outcome just as a committee member. Drafts of sections of Chapters 2, 3, and 4 were prepared at the committee's request by David P. Campbell, Morris H. DeGroot, Charles B. Perrow, Sherwood L. Washburn, and Julian Wolpert. Others assisted in the review and revision of the report and papers: Brian J. L. Berry, Key Dismukes, John Ferejohn, Morris Fiorina, Rod Gretlein, Robert Hennessy, Gerald Kramer, Robert J. Lapham, David Philbean, Michael I. Posner, W. Richard Scott, Susan W. Sherman, Russell Tuttle, and Alexandra K. Wigdor. William H. Kruskal read and commented on an earlier draft of the entire report. Roberta Balstad Miller, of the SSRC staff, closely cooperated with the committee in the selection and securing of the three commissioned papers for which there was some joint responsibility.

Donald J. Treiman served as study director for this undertaking from its inception, extending his leave from UCLA in order to do so. The organization and administration of the effort rested largely on his shoulders, and the smoothness and effectiveness of the committee's functioning should be credited in large part to him. Always subject to the candid, perceptive, and sometimes devastating criticisms of the committee, he, Neil Smelser, and I shared primary responsibility for writing of successive drafts. It has been a highly pleasurable as well as educational experience to work with both of them on successive iterations, our—or at any rate my—appreciation of the issues changing as well as deepening in the process. Both personally and on behalf of the committee as a whole, I should like to acknowledge a special debt of gratitude to Treiman for a major contribution, without which this report might not have been possible.

Thanks are also owing to other members of the National Research Council staff. Patricia A. Roos served as research associate to the committee, ably assisting in the coordination of its work until taking up an academic position in September 1981. Rose S. Kaufman was most helpful as the committee's administrative secretary, thoughtfully arranging the details of its meetings and typing its report. David A. Goslin, executive director of the Commission on Behavioral and Social Sciences and Education, and Eugenia Grohman, associate director for reports for the Commission, read earlier drafts of the report and made many valuable suggestions. Christine L. McShane, editor for the Commission, has made a significant contribution in matters of substance as well as style. Dean R. Gerstein, who will succeed Treiman as study director upon submission of this report, offered useful criticisms during the final editing and coordinated the completion of the commissioned papers.

Finally, it is a pleasure to record my thanks to the committee as a whole for its common acceptance and collegial execution of a challenging responsibility. Perhaps there was some initial floundering before we found ways to articulate the separate outlooks and bodies of experience that we brought to the assignment, but the discourse that quickly evolved was as balanced, mutually considerate and consistently constructive as it was wide-ranging. One sometimes hears dismissals of studies like this as "only" committee reports, and sometimes such negative appraisals are justified. But a task like this one could not have been undertaken without the cooperative effort of a group. And I cannot imagine that a stronger, more critical, and yet also more harmonious group could have been induced to come together and do it.

ROBERT MCC. ADAMS, *Chair*
Committee on Basic Research in
the Behavioral and Social Sciences

Contents

1 Introduction

The Committee on Basic Research in the Behavioral and Social Sciences was formed in response to a request from the National Science Foundation to the National Academy of Sciences-National Research Council; that request was for a report that would:

- Specify appropriate criteria for assessing the value, significance, and social utility of basic research in the social sciences;
- Identify illustrative areas of basic research in the social sciences that have developed analytic frameworks of high social utility and describe the development of these frameworks and their utilization;
- Identify illustrative areas of basic research in the social sciences that are likely to be of high value, significance, and/or social utility in the near future, review the current state of knowledge in these areas, and indicate research efforts needed to bring these areas to their full potential; and
- Serve as a model for social scientists in presenting the potential implications and value of basic research in areas not included in the illustrations in this report.

Although this formal charge refers to the social sciences, the committee understands its responsibility to encompass what is usually included in the behavioral and social sciences.

VALUE, SIGNIFICANCE, AND SOCIAL UTILITY

Central to the committee's charge is the phrase *value, significance, and social utility*. Our task was to assess basic research in the behavioral and social

1

sciences in light of these three criteria. We regard them not as mutually exclusive but rather as overlapping and complementary; at the same time, each is a distinctive prism through which the same set of research activities or findings may appear different. By basic research in the behavioral and social sciences, we mean research that has as its primary aim the understanding and explanation of human behavior and social arrangements. Basic research can be most simply defined as the discovery of new knowledge. As a result of basic research, empirically verified descriptions and explanations of natural phenomena and laws that govern their occurrence and interrelations are systematically accumulated.

Value calls to mind intrinsic desirability and degree of excellence, although its other connotations (such as a fair return and relative worth) may imply a need to weigh quality against cost. *Significance* emphasizes importance in a wider sense, as in research contributions that subsequently play an essential part in other, perhaps originally unassociated, disciplines or applications. *Social utility* points primarily in the direction of the well-being of individuals, groups, and society as a whole. This report stresses that the full range of utility extends well beyond both practical applications and public policies. So described, the three terms encompass a spectrum from the advancement of narrowly defined research goals at one end to a ramifying potential for individual and social betterment at the other.

Of the three terms, *value* probably can be defined least ambiguously. Value represents a judgment about the research process itself—the importance and timeliness of the problem addressed, the soundness of methodological innovations, the richness and reliability of data, and the superiority or originality of the conceptual framework. These criteria of value are central to judgments made by scientists in all fields. Academic appointments and promotions, review of manuscripts for publication, and peer review of proposals for research are all devices for implementing them. In each case there is a central judgment about an individual's or a group's accomplishment or about a problem around which further research can be organized: To what extent has it contributed, or is it likely to contribute, to the enhancement of scientific knowledge? Such a question presupposes—as does the committee— that the systematic pursuit of knowledge for its own sake is an essential contribution to the betterment of the human condition.

Moving beyond the value criterion, the report addresses the other two criteria by posing a second basic question: What are the contributions of scientific knowledge beyond the normal boundaries of the discipline or disciplines that created it? That available knowledge has always been brought into service for wider, often directly practical ends is clear. With its aid, ways are found to do things more efficiently, to create new goods and services, to inform decision making, and to improve the quality of life as well as, of course, contribute to the advancement of knowledge in other scientific disciplines through the diffusion of methods, instruments, and theories. Knowledge about human behavior and institutions is not different in these respects from other kinds of knowledge. On this as well as other grounds, it is the committee's conviction that the behavioral and social sciences must be judged by the same criteria as other sciences. In short, the justification for basic research in all fields lies in the knowledge-generating utility of scientific discoveries and in the well-founded anticipation—but not guarantee—that some of those discoveries will in the long run prove to be of great practical benefit.

ORGANIZATION OF THE REPORT

The committee has approached its task in two ways. First, we commissioned a set of papers to review various research areas or topics in the behavioral and social sciences that have had great payoff or that show considerable promise. In some instances the payoff has been in the form of discoveries or inventions of practical value, while in others it has been in the form of advancement in understanding of ourselves and our society. These papers constitute Part II of a supplement to the committee's report (see Appendix A for the contents of Part II). Second, the report itself suggests criteria for assessing the value, significance, and social utility of basic research in the behavioral and social sciences and illustrates these criteria with examples drawn from recent research, including the topics reviewed in the papers.

The body of the report, comprising the committee's response to its charge, is divided into four chapters. Chapter 2 considers the subject matter and modes of research activity in the behavioral and social sciences. The chapter first provides a general map of how the research terrain has been divided among different disciplines and gives an account of the dynamics of the process by which traditional lines of specialization and complementary theoretical and methodological emphases have developed. It then goes on to consider the varieties of theory and method that characterize the behavioral and social sciences. Different sources of data are mentioned, as are the means by which investigators typically analyze them.

Chapter 3 illustrates the progress of the behavioral and social sciences as sciences, reviewing a number of areas in which significant advances in knowledge have been made in recent years. One striking feature of these advances is that frequently they have been borrowed from or have contributed to other disciplines, often outside the behavioral and social sciences. Sociologists who have inquired into the dynamics of social mobility and status attainment, for example, have made liberal use of statistical methods developed by geneticists and econometricians. Another example is the study of human perception, which has involved a long-term interaction between psychophysicists describing behavior and sensory physiologists describing the physiological substrate of that behavior; this collaboration is documented in the paper by Braida et al. (in Part II).

Chapter 4 describes a variety of applications of research findings to public policy formation and social problem solving as well as more diffuse processes by which knowledge from the behavioral and social sciences contributes to society. Our illustrations range widely and include the reformulation of lay understanding in areas such as racial differences; improvements in productivity and individual well-being through human factors and organizational design; and the invention of information-gathering technologies, such as survey research, that have improved the ability of society to monitor the information necessary for planning and governance in a complex democracy.

Chapter 5 sets forth in more general terms the committee's view of the relationship between basic research and its influence and practical application. We understand this relationship as a continuum, with influence running in reciprocal directions and without hard-and-fast distinctions as to how problems are perceived or how work is organized. We regard the process of application as simultaneously technical, social, and political; as a result, considerable lags occur between specialized advances in knowledge and their wider employment. In addition, new and unexpected connections arise in the process, and it is difficult if not impossible to estimate in advance the influence or importance of a particular area of basic research.

This chapter also presents the conclusions of the committee. The most fundamental of these is that basic research in the behavioral and social sciences—like basic research in other disciplines—should be regarded as a long-term investment in social capital. The benefits to society of such an investment are significant and lasting, although often not immediate or obvious. A steep reduction in the investment may produce short-run savings, but it would be likely to have damaging long-term consequences for the well-being of the nation and its citizens.

RELATIONSHIP OF THIS REPORT TO PREVIOUS STUDIES

Many previous studies have dealt with various aspects of social research and its uses. These include a number of general reports by broadly representative committees of specialists as well as the voluminous writings of individuals. We cannot provide a comprehensive listing of the very numerous and diverse individual contributions on the subject, but the major committee reports include:

- National Research Council (1968) *The Behavioral Sciences and the Federal Government* (Young report).
- National Research Council and Social Science Research Council (1969) *The Behavioral and Social Sciences: Outlook and Needs* (BASS report).
- National Science Board (1969) *Knowledge Into Action: Improving the Nation's Use of the Social Sciences* (Brim report).
- National Research Council (1976) *Social and Behavioral Science Programs in the National Science Foundation* (Simon report).
- National Research Council (Kiesler and Turner, eds., 1977) *Fundamental Research and the Process of Education.*
- National Research Council (1978) *The Federal Investment in Knowledge of Social Problems.*

These reports, while differing somewhat among themselves, also differ in their concerns from the present one. Most of them rest on the premise that the behavioral and social sciences can and should play a substantial part in solving social problems. The Young report, for example, was primarily concerned with ways to improve the use of social research by agencies of the federal government in making policy. The BASS report includes a set of individual volumes that assessed the status and needs of particular behavioral and social sciences; its main report not only called for increased federal support for the social and behavioral sciences but also made a number of suggestions for improving the linkages among the various disciplines and between the social science community and the government. This report also proposed the creation of a set of social indicators corresponding to economic indicators. As the title *Knowledge Into Action* indicates, the Brim report spoke to many of these same concerns. The Simon report had a somewhat more specific focus, calling for a reorganization of social and behavioral science programs within the National Science Foundation, while on the whole supporting the quality and effectiveness of these programs. The report on fundamental research in education proposed a shift in federal support of educational research toward more basic research. And the report on the federal investment in knowledge of social problems had a still different character, devoting considerable attention to the policy-making process and stressing the limitations of social research as a tool for making social policy or for operating social programs.

Many of the analyses and proposals in these studies still deserve serious attention as guides for policy. None of them, however, was directly concerned with assessing the value, significance, or social utility of basic research— indeed, none of them treated basic research in the behavioral and social sciences as problematic in this respect. Hence, the charge given to this committee has led to a report with substantially different content and objectives from previous efforts under similar auspices.

THE BEHAVIORAL AND SOCIAL SCIENCES

The behavioral and social sciences are those parts of a number of organized academic and applied disciplines that have as a common objective the explanation of the behavior and social relations of human beings by the application of scientific methods.

As distinctive disciplines, the behavioral and social sciences are a development of the late 19th century. During this period the first academic departments were established, the first journals were published, and the first professional societies in the disciplines of anthropology, economics, geography, psychology, political science, and sociology were founded. These fields still constitute the core of social science divisions in most colleges and universities today, sometimes together with history, which is variously regarded as a social science and as a humanistic discipline.

To equate the behavioral and social sciences with these named disciplines, however, is imprecise for at least two reasons. First, like other scientific disciplines, these fields are constantly subdividing and realigning as new knowledge, techniques, and problems shift the focus of attention and suggest the desirability of communication with colleagues from what were initially other disciplines. For example, demography, the study of the size and distribution of human populations, has emerged as a distinct discipline yet still draws most of its students from among those who also identify themselves as sociologists, economists, and biologists. A similar point can be made about sociolinguistics, the study of the interpersonal and social determinants and consequences of language use, a discipline that draws on anthropology, psychology, sociology, and philosophy, as well as the field of linguistics, itself a derivative of philology, and to some extent anthropology. The new field of cognitive science, the study of human thinking, straddles areas of psychology, biology, and computer science. And so on—the list of such examples is very long. Each field continually spawns new subspecialties as its knowledge base increases. A list of some of the subspecialties of economics, which have developed in addition to the major division of the field into microeconomic theory and macroeconomic theory, illustrates this point: mathematical economic theory, econometrics, the history of economic thought, economic history, economic development, industrial organization, agricultural economics, labor economics, public finance, international economics, consumer economics, comparative economics, welfare economics, and regional economics (Rees, 1968:4.482-4.484). Many of these specialties also overlap with work in other disciplines.

Second, the social and behavioral sciences provide the research underpinnings for all or part of several applied fields. In medicine, psychosocial factors are now strongly implicated in the etiology of some diseases and disorders and in the efficacy of treatment (see the papers in Part II by Krantz et al. on behavior and health and by Wilson on behavioral therapy). The legal profession has increasingly engaged in and been influenced by social science research on the impact of regulatory laws and agencies, laws against pornography, the interaction between the incidence of crime and patterns of arrest, trial, and punishment, and the behavior of judges and juries. Basic research in the behavioral and social sciences provides much of the empirical base for the practices and principles promulgated in schools of business, education, urban planning, public health, international affairs, public administration, and social welfare. And research in these fields often contributes to the stock of basic knowledge. Finally, many fields of study—mathematics, statistics, and computer science, for example—have been stimulated by research questions in the social and behavioral sciences to develop particularly suitable models, methods, and techniques.

Despite the imperfect fit between established academic disciplines and behavioral and social science activities as a whole, for the sake of convenience we use these disciplinary labels as the basis for organizing a brief description of the concerns and methods of the behavioral and social sciences. That is the task of the next chapter.

2 The Nature and Methods of the Behavioral and Social Sciences

Common sense suggests that there are various kinds of facts, and that every field of inquiry selects distinctive kinds of facts for its focus. Biological sciences, for example, focus on bodily functions such as respiration, circulation, and metabolism in organisms and on the relations of organisms with their environments. Psychological sciences focus on drives, perceptions, beliefs, and other facts relating to personality. Sociology focuses on friendships, group memberships, social standings, and occupations.

On closer examination, however, this compartmentalized view of academic disciplines is not an accurate one. The same fact or event can be of interest to a number of disciplines. Take a particular event—the decision of a woman to seek a job outside the home. Most social scientists would be relatively uninterested in the particular decision of a particular woman but would formulate research questions in terms of accounting for why some women work outside the home while others do not and why women have been entering the labor force in increasing numbers in recent years.

In addressing these questions, researchers in the different disciplines would tend to focus on different factors and would make use of different data; indeed, the definition of what constitutes data depends on the conceptualization of the problem. Economists might ask whether increases in the demand for labor have increased pay rates and would compare the value of potential income from employment with the value of the work women do at home and the value of their leisure. Sociologists might focus on changes in the kinds of jobs available to women and on family patterns that put the major responsibility for household maintenance on wives and encourage them to defer to their husbands' career needs. Psychologists might ask what role work outside the household plays in a woman's self-image and sense of self-worth, how these feelings are created, and how they are changing. And demographers might concentrate on the effect of trends in the birth rate on the demand for particular goods and services and on the supply of labor. In short, what mainly distinguishes academic disciplines from one another is not that they focus on different kinds of facts but rather that they interpret the same facts within distinctive conceptual frameworks.

So, while in what follows we speak of kinds of facts, it is important to remember that they are invoked as facts in the context of a certain conceptual framework. It is also important to realize that these conceptual frameworks are constantly changing, as a natural adjunct to the development of new knowledge, which creates the danger that any attempt to identify the core problems of each discipline will be immediately out of date. Moreover, these fields overlap substantially, and the same problems are often addressed by researchers from different disciplines. For example, the relationship between attitudes and behavior is a problem of social psychology, which is regarded as a subspecialty of both psychology and sociology; various questions regarding employment and earnings are of interest to both sociologists and economists; voting is studied by both political scientists and sociologists; and so on. Keeping these clarifications and caveats in mind, we proceed now to identify the central concerns of the individual behavioral and social science disciplines.

THE BEHAVIORAL AND SOCIAL SCIENCE DISCIPLINES

PSYCHOLOGY

We begin with psychology, which can be defined as the scientific study of behavior. The term *behavior* is used broadly and includes all responses of humans (and other animals)—overt motor acts and physiological responses (such as heart beat and blood pressure) as well as mental events. Behavior includes both external, easily observable actions and events that can be inferred only indirectly from verbal reports or from physiological indicators, such as changes in heart rate. Psychologists study how behavior patterns are acquired, how they are maintained over time, how they are modified, how they are suppressed, abandoned, or forgotten, and how particular responses that are parts of these patterns occur under particular circumstances. Psychological research tends to focus on the behavior of the individual organism—in the case of humans, the individual person—as the primary unit of analysis, in contrast to the social sciences, which tend to focus on relations among people (e.g., roles, the division of labor, power relationships) and on relational systems (e.g., market systems, governmental strategies, residential patterns).

Over the past 50 years, psychology has grown rapidly and has become differentiated into a number of complementary specialties (although they overlap to some extent). The methods and approaches to studying behavior vary with the specialty. Psychologists who are interested in learning, for example, study behavior—any behavior—as it is influenced by repetition under different regimes of rewards and punishments. Psychologists who are interested in sensation and perception analyze how individuals perceive stimuli that impinge on their senses; the paper on psychophysics by Braida et al. (in Part II) illustrates this focus. Physiological psychologists attempt to explain behavioral regularities in terms of physiological and neurochemical processes and structures with a primary emphasis on brain-behavior relations. Cognitive psychologists view behavior as a consequence of internal processes that occur as the individual acquires, manipulates, and retains information; the paper on reading as a cognitive process by Carpenter and Just (in Part II) is an example of the cognitive focus. Other specialties employ the fundamental knowledge and methods of these fields to understand behavior in group settings (social psychology) and long-term changes in and stability of behavior (developmental and life-span psychology); an illustration of the latter is Nelson's paper on early cognitive development (in Part II). Personality psychologists and psychometricians investigate stable differences among individuals in their predispositions, skills, and abilities and develop diagnostic instruments for identifying psychopathology and psychological disability. Another field, psychometrics, largely overlaps with statistics; this area is described more fully in the section below on statistics. Among the specialties of applied psychology are clinical, consulting, counseling, educational, industrial, organizational, engineering, consumer, health, military, pastoral, environmental psychology, and psychopharmacology.

SOCIOLOGY

Sociology is the study of social organization. By this is meant the way human societies and their constituent parts are organized. Sociologists take as their subject matter what members of a society ordinarily take for granted: How and why it is that most people generally behave in an orderly way (we stake our lives on this assumption each time we get into an automobile); how standards of appropriate behavior are learned and come to be shared; how behavior is governed by social relationships (such as employee-boss, husband-wife, buyer-seller) and what the elements of such relationships are— reciprocity, dominance, power, trust, loyalty, etc.; how, why, and with what consequences society's rewards and resources (power, privilege, prestige) are distributed across social categories defined by sex, age, race, or other attributes; how basic social needs are met through the institutions of family, work, education, politics, religion, etc., and how these institutions change over time and vary across societies.

The units sociologists study range from pairs of interacting individuals to entire societies, and the range of analytic perspectives is very large. A few examples suffice to give a taste of this diversity. The demographic perspective emphasizes the distribution of the characteristics of social aggregates or populations. Age and sex distributions and their relations to the size and growth of populations are the concerns of formal demography, which, as was mentioned in the previous chapter, has become a distinct discipline (see the paper by Menken and Trussell in Part II). But a broader demographic perspective within sociology leads to a focus on the interrelations among such social characteristics as education, occupation, income, race, and place of residence as well as age and sex. A social psychological perspective leads to concern with such questions as how people interact in small groups, how attitudes are formed, how society and personality interact in the process of socialization, and how beliefs are formed and spread in episodes of collective behavior, such as panics or riots. The macrohistorical perspective emphasizes overarching principles of societal organization and their consequences and leads to the study of large-scale social change. Comparisons between feudal, capitalist, and socialist economies, analyses of the rise of the nation-state, and studies of the social impact of multinational corporations are examples of research informed by this perspective. A final example is the cultural perspective. This includes the study of cosmologies, value systems, and normative patterns that regulate, justify, and give meaning to social behavior. More concretely, it involves sociologists in the study of religious systems, legal systems, informal norms, and high and mass culture.

As with other fields, much of sociology is oriented toward analyzing issues of contemporary concern. This has led to the proliferation of subfields that to some extent crosscut the perspectives outlined above. Some are identified by the major institutions of society they study—the sociology of religion, medicine, or education. Some refer to the major types of groups in society— the sociology of small groups or formal organizations. Some refer to some kind of social process, as in the sociology of deviance or social movements. And some are named after the social problems on which they focus—for example, the sociology of mental illness or poverty.

ANTHROPOLOGY

Considered as a whole, anthropology is customarily divided into four major subfields. The first is physical anthropology, which involves the biological characteristics of human beings as influenced by heredity and environment and which occasions the study of fossil remains of primates and humans as well as the study of the biological characteristics and behavior of primates; physical anthropology overlaps with paleontology, biology, and the other life sciences. The second is archaeology, which involves the recovery (largely through excavations) and study of the material remains of former cultures. There is again substantial overlap and interaction with the physical and biologial sciences. Not only does this serve in part to increase the recovery of what is inevitably fragmentary evidence, but it also assists in broadening the interpretation of patterns of human activity and their environmental contexts. Archaeology also overlaps substantially with history and other humanistic disciplines, at least in the study of past cultures for which a historical record exists. The third is linguistic anthropology, which overlaps with linguistic studies in many social sciences and humanities and involves the study of vocabularies, grammars, systems of usage, and patterns of change in the languages of cultures.

Finally, there is sociocultural anthropology (alternately called, with differences in nuance, social anthropology, cultural anthropology, or ethnology), in which most anthropologists specialize. It maintains an inclusive focus on the contemporary and relatively recent cultures of the world, with particular respect to social organization, interpersonal relations, and systems of traditional values or beliefs and patterned activities. Within sociocultural anthropology there are further subdivisions—for example, economic anthropology and legal anthropology. Psychological anthropology (sometimes referred to as the study of culture and personality) bears similarity to parts of social psychology, with some differences in theoretical emphasis. As mentioned, some social anthropologists include demographic studies in their repertoire; the paper on land tenure by Netting (in Part II) illustrates an ecological approach that has also assumed some prominence. Others are mainly concerned with systematized areas of belief and behavior, such as myth and ritual (see, for example, the paper by D'Andrade in Part II).

What, then, are the differences between sociology and sociocultural anthropology? Because of their different origins—anthropology arising in historical coincidence with the colonizing and missionary spread of the West to other parts of the world, and sociology arising in connection with the fundamental transformations in the West of the industrial and democratic revolutions—anthropologists and sociologists traditionally have studied social life in different settings. Anthropologists have concentrated on small, simple, often nonliterate societies, whereas sociologists have mainly studied large, complex, literate civilizations. Particularly in the past two decades, however, this distinction has been breaking down, as both sociologists and anthropologists study caste in Indian villages, as anthropologists take up investigations of places like East London, and as sociologists broaden their comparative scope. Moreover, although anthropologists tend to focus on cultural values and meaning systems more than do sociologists, the interest of sociologists in art, literature, religion, and mass culture qualifies this generalization. While anthropological research has centered on certain institutional aspects, such as kinship, magic, and religion, that have been thought to infuse simpler societies, these subjects are not without interest to sociologists; by the same token, especially in modern times, anthropologists have interested themselves in economic structure, political structure, stratification, economic develop-ment, and other aspects of social life. Finally, both anthropologists and sociologists have recently come to take a greater interest in history and the work of historians.

ECONOMICS

In contrast to the relative breadth and inclusiveness characterizing the behavioral and social sciences mentioned so far, economics has a sharper and more delimited disciplinary focus. It concentrates on how individuals— and society as a whole—choose to use scarce resources to produce various commodities and distribute them for consumption among individuals and groups. This general concern involves several more specialized issues.

The first set of issues is indicated by the term *commodities*. What is the level of the total production of goods and services in a society? What different kinds of commodities are produced, and in what proportions? Economists attempt to account for variations in the level and composition of production. The second set of issues arises from the term *scarce resources*. Goods and services are produced by the application of the following factors of production: (1) land, or the level and kind of available natural resources and the cultural values and technical knowledge that govern their use; (2) labor, or the level of motivation and skill of human beings; (3) capital, or the level of resources available for future production rather than immediate consumption; and, sometimes, (4) organization, or the principles involved in the combination and recombination of the other factors. Economists are interested in explaining the levels and relative proportions of these resources in productive use and the techniques by which they are combined. The third set of issues is suggested by the term *distribute*. Which individuals and groups receive the goods and services generated in the production process? Or, to put it in terms of payment, what is the distribution of income generated in the economic process?

Economists are interested in the forces that determine the level and composition of production, the allocation of resources, and the distribution of wealth. What are these forces? In broad terms, economists recognize mechanisms such as religious decrees, customary arrangements, and political arrangements, but formal economic analysis has traditionally stressed supply and demand in the market as the immediate mechanism. The level and composition of production depend on the desires of different individuals and groups for products and the conditions under which producers are willing to supply them. The level and composition of the factors of production depend on the relationship between the demand for them on the part of producers and the difficulties and costs involved in securing them. Finally, the proportions of income received by different individuals and groups depend on the conditions of supply and demand governing the relations among economic agents. At the same time, economists have also noted environmental causes and consequences of the behavior of markets.

In developing these kinds of explanations, economists have tended to focus on two levels of analysis. Microeconomics has to do with specifying the preferences and assumptions of economic agents (consumers and producers, households and firms, etc.) and analyzing how these assumptions and preferences influence the behavior of those agents and thus constitute conditions of demand and supply, which generate various economic outcomes. Outcomes are thought to depend on such factors as the degree to which agents' knowledge is certain or uncertain, the degree to which "public goods" (goods that are freely available to everyone once they are developed, such as environmental improvements) enter the market, and the degree to which agents are free from regulation or other constraints (see the discussion on resource allocation in Chapter 4 for specific examples). An example of microeconomic analysis is found in the paper by Heckman and Michael (in Part II) on income distribution, poverty, and labor mobility. Macroeconomics, by contrast, concerns the study of entire economies and involves aggregating or averaging individual units into some kind of total level of a society's employment, investment, national income, and so on. Macroeconomics studies the regularities in the movement and relations among these aggregated totals.

Like the other behavioral and social sciences, economics has been divided into a range of subspecialties. Some deal with the analysis of a special factor of production: For example, the analysis of money and banking focuses on the structure and dynamics of money, capital, and credit in the economy, while labor economics is the specialized study of conditions affecting that particular factor. Other specialties vary according to the scope of analysis covered—for example, regional economics, national economics, and international economics. Still others refer to kinds of economic processes, such as economic development. Finally, economics has a number of applied fields, such as urban economics, agricultural economics, and economics of the public sector, which focus on problems, constraints, and policy questions in the areas indicated. A subspecialty in economics that cuts across a number of substantive areas is econometrics, the development of statistical procedures for the measurement and analysis of economic phenomena. This subspecialty is described below in the section on the field of statistics, and some additional examples of its application are given in the section on economic data and economic models in Chapter 4.

POLITICAL SCIENCE

Political science is in certain respects parallel to economics analytically, in that it deals with the creation, organization, and use of a distinctive social commodity—power (analogous to wealth in economics). A second point of parallelism is that the production and organization of power can be said to be a function of the combination of a number of scarce resources—especially legitimacy, public support, administrative skill, and financial resources. Despite these similarities, however, political science as a discipline is to a degree less definitely focused than economics. Among other reasons, this has to do with the fact that political scientists—like sociologists and anthropologists—have not arrived at a general consensus on concepts as specific as supply and demand to account for how power is produced, distributed, and exercised.

The investigation of power depends, of course, on the normative rules that guide the use of power in a society. Not surprisingly, American political science has been largely concerned with how the doctrine of constitutional democracy operates in American society. The theory of democracy has been gradually expanded and deepened as a result of empirical studies of elections, political parties, public participation, public opinion, legislative behavior, and so forth.

One tradition of political science is concerned with describing and analyzing formal political institutions at different political and geographical levels. American government, for example, customarily has been viewed as an account of how American political institutions such as the Constitution, statutory law, and customary practices (for example, party behavior) work. Traditional treatments of state governments, federal-state relations, and county and municipal governments are similarly concerned with the workings of political institutions, as is the traditional approach to international relations, except that the latter has also been characterized in part by an emphasis on diplomatic history. In these traditional areas of political science, the literature is also concerned with policy implications—for example, the pros and cons of various forms of municipal government, such as council-mayor, commission, and city manager. Another offshoot of this tradition is comparative government. Preoccupied in earlier decades with Western constitutional governments and large-scale political institutions, it extends more recently into the study and analysis of socialist and communist forms of government as well as the emerging systems of governments, parties, and political arrangements in the less developed countries of the world.

In the postwar decades, especially the 1950s and early 1960s, two new approaches emerged in political science: the *behavioral* approach and the *functional* approach. These decades witnessed an increased interest in empirical (as contrasted with normative) analysis of political behavior and institutions as well as the borrowing, modification, and application of then-dominant models from the other behavioral and social sciences, especially psychology and sociology. The behavioral approach tended to concentrate more on the behavior of individuals in political situations and less on the formal structure of political institutions, explaining individual behavior by reference to social and psychological determinants. Voting behavior, for example, was shown to be influenced by race, education, socioeconomic class, religion, and family as well as by various psychological variables such as level of political consciousness and political commitment (see the paper on voting research by Converse et al. in Part II). The functional approach involved a concentration on the polity as a system, emphasizing the mutual interrelations among the various groups, structures, and processes within that system. In addition, that approach spawned a much more comprehensive comparative scope and began to study the political structure and functioning of various kinds of groups and structures that had not previously been considered as primarily political—tribes, clans, and other kinship groups, for example. The behavioral-functional impetus has also given rise to comparative studies—under the heading of cross-national studies—that systematically investigate the functional relations among different kinds of political phenomena, such as the type of state and the level of political violence as well as the relations between political structures and processes and other kinds of social and economic phenomena.

Despite the increased emphasis on the empirical approach and the great kaleidoscope of approaches to the study of power, political science has retained a consistent emphasis on public policy analysis, and, along with economics, it stands out in this regard from the other behavioral and social sciences. This policy emphasis involves not only the evaluation of political arrangements and decisions but also the *processes* by which policy decisions are generated, made, and implemented (or deflected). Furthermore, the policy stress is found in the study of all levels of political life—local, national, and international.

Geography

Although geography has a component of physical science and overlaps with a number of earth sciences, especially geology and meteorology, it is now primarily and increasingly concerned with social science questions. Recently, however, some geographers have returned to the traditional concern with problems of ecology, environmental deterioration, adaptations to risk, and energy.

Basic research in human geography has been focused on two major types of issues: the relationships between people and the environment and spatial theories of location and movement. Research in the environmental tradition has developed and used a variety of behavioral models to examine the human imprint on landscape, the use and conservation of the physical environment, the development of resources, and the perception of and response to natural hazards. Environmental geographers are interested in the forces that affect the development and use of land and water for agriculture, grazing, and recreation, the characteristics of landscape that are valued and preserved, and the manifestations of uncertainty and risk in land use. The geographer uses the earth's landscape as laboratory, both to test basic social science and physical science theories and to provide comparative observations for the development of new theory. Much of the recent advancement in our understanding of people's tolerance of, aversion to, and management of risk, for example, has come from studies of flood insurance and the impacts of droughts and earthquakes.

Geographers and regional scientists whose research focuses on spatial analysis study regional development and decline, the size and spacing of settlements, interregional population redistribution, processes of suburbanization, and industrial siting. They also examine such topics as the structure of urban land use, the provision and delivery of public services, and the relationship of land use to transportation systems.

History

It is difficult to contrast history, defined most generally as the discipline that attempts an accurate account and understanding of the past, with the other social sciences with respect to subject matter, because in principle history shares a common mass of raw data with the other social science disciplines.

Not only are people, societies, and institutions the common focus of all the social sciences, but history also borrows freely from its sister disciplines. A historian seeking to date an early Mississippi settlement and a medievalist seeking to discover the steps in building cathedrals both employ the hypotheses and techniques of archaeology to date the timbers and the stones. A modern explanation for the economic collapse of the western European part of the Roman Empire uses the theories of the latest regional and international trade economics.

Conversely, other social sciences borrow frequently from historical research. Much of the improved quality of today's demographic sociology rests on the efforts of historians to evaluate and detect errors in the population records of the past. The focus of modern political history on revolutions, the nation-state and its institutions, and industrialization reveals the overlap of historical and political science research in both data and concepts. One might note as well that at this moment the economic rationale of the policies of the governments of both the United States and the United Kingdom rests on hypotheses drawn from a history of the money supply in the United States.

The vagueness of boundary is made even more elusive by the fact that many historians do not seek to practice social science at all, but rather follow a very old and very popular branch of literature. The chronicle, the biography, and the narrative—the most common forms of historical research and writing—neither propose nor test any hypotheses, but instead follow the canons of these forms of literature.

Historians who do regard themselves as social scientists are distinguished from social scientists in other disciplines by several features. Historians tend to concentrate on material that is recorded relatively far in the past. They also tend to organize their subject matter in somewhat different ways. As a rule they use three criteria to subdivide their field: chronological time, cultural and/or national tradition, and aspects of social life. The familiar phrases "British social history of the 19th century" and "western European intellectual history during the 18th century" exemplify these criteria. Other social scientists tend to use more abstract and formal categories—consumption, social structure, and value patterns, for example—to subdivide their disciplines.

In part because historians must depend for evidence on the surviving fragments of the past, both artifacts and written records, the selection of data influences their specialty. Any hypothesis to be tested must find its validation in what survives; the pressure of the evidence tends to make historians identify their intellectual problems and their causes and explanations differently from their fellow social scientists.

STATISTICS

Like geography and history, statistics is only partially a social science. It differs from these disciplines, however, in that it is involved not with substance but with methods. We include it because statistical methods form the basis for the analytic procedures on which a great portion of research in the behavioral and social sciences depends, and these procedures were developed in substantial part to solve problems in this research.

The science of statistics deals with the development of methods that are appropriate for making inferences and decisions under the conditions of uncertainty and partial ignorance that necessarily exist in a wide range of human activities. Modern statistical practice depends mainly on the formulation of probability models of social and physical systems, on methods of collecting and analyzing numerical data, and on the design of efficient and informative experiments.

Statistical science as we know it today is largely a development of the 20th century. The ground-breaking work in England during the first three decades of the century was stimulated largely by problems in agriculture and genetics. Subsequent pioneering work during the next two decades was carried out in response to economic problems and the exigencies of World War II. The past three decades have witnessed a rapid expansion of the theory and applications of statistics; today statistical methods are an important part of most areas of science, technology, and management. In particular, because of the wide variety of data that can be collected about human behavior, the apparent stochastic nature of much of these data (that is, the fact that they involve random or chance elements), and our inherent interest in analyzing them in order to learn about ourselves as humans and as a society, statistics and probability pervade virtually all fields of research in the behavioral and social sciences. This section is a brief survey of the diverse ways they have been used in these fields.

The field of econometrics comprises a wide collection of statistical models and methods that have been found applicable in problems of empirical economics. Research in econometrics includes methods for developing statistical models of economic time series, including large-scale models of the U.S. economy (see Chapter 4), and methods for developing forecasts based on these models. Statistics are fundamental in measuring employment and unemployment, in establishing economic indices such as the consumer price index, and in determining and forecasting trends in these measures. They are used in predicting and measuring the effects of changes in taxation and the money supply and of other governmental policies on the economy. The theories of probability and statistics play an important part in modern economic theory. The concepts of subjective probability and Bayesian statistics (Savage, 1954) have been used in the development of models of duopoly and oligopoly and are basic to the extensive research currently being carried out in the area of rational expectations. Econometric models and methods have also been used in the field of history, to study, for example, the economic effects of slavery in the United States.

In psychology, the field of psychometrics has long been concerned with a body of general statistical methods that are of particular use in that discipline. Statistical methods of test calibration, for example, are essential for comparing different versions of ability tests such as the Scholastic Aptitude Test and for detecting shifts in test scores over time. Probability models form the basic framework for analysis in the area of learning processes. A current research area in which psychology, probability, and statistics interact and nourish each other is the study of how people form subjective probabilities, how they change these probabilities in light of new information, and how they use these probabilities in decision making (Tversky and Kahneman, 1981). Statistics also supports and stimulates much research in the areas of psychiatry and mental health.

Statistical surveys to measure public attitudes and other social characteristics of interest are today essential tools of sociology and the social sciences in general (see Chapter 4). The work of Hansen, Hurwitz, and Madow (1953) laid the statistical foundations for virtually all of the surveys carried out by the U.S. Bureau of the Census and other government agencies in the past 30 years and through these agencies has essentially shaped current survey methodology. In the area of criminal justice, statistics and probability pervade almost every facet of study. Surveys, panel data, and other statistical methods are used to estimate victimization rates and the frequencies of different types of crimes as well as to forecast trends. Probability models of criminal behavior and of the effects of incarceration and various sentencing policies have been developed. Statistical methods have been used to help cities determine the optimal use and deployment of their police and fire-fighting forces. Probability and statistics have been used to develop fair ways of drawing prospective jurors from a community and to help trial lawyers use their peremptory challenges optimally when selecting a jury. Statistical models and statistical evidence are an important part of most court cases involving race, sex, or age discrimination as well as of antitrust cases and hearings before regulatory agencies involving the setting of utility rates. Other branches of sociology, such as social networks, are based almost entirely on the development of probability models and their statistical analysis.

In demography, stochastic processes are used for modeling population growth and changes and for forecasting these changes. Statistical methodology is basic to the planning, design, and analysis of the decennial census in the United States. Statistical methods are used to obtain estimates of the undercount of various subgroups of the population, and they provide a theoretical framework for making adjustments for this undercount. In political science, statistical models of voting patterns and voting behavior in popular elections, legislative bodies, international assemblies, and other forums have been developed. Election forecasts during the period preceding an election and during election night on television have become a familiar part of our lives. They are usually followed by a statistical analysis of election results to help determine which subgroups of the electorate voted for certain candidates or certain issues.

Finally, there is the field of decision analysis, in which principles of economics, psychology, management, engineering, and statistical decision theory have been brought together to aid decision makers in a wide variety of contexts, including government policy. Much of this work deals with methods for specifying probabilities, utilities, and available alternatives in complex decision problems involving a large number of variables and multiple objectives.

DYNAMICS OF DEVELOPMENT IN THE BEHAVIORAL AND SOCIAL SCIENCES

A general map of the subject matter of the main behavioral and social science disciplines, like all maps, is likely to be misleading because it is a kind of cross-sectional photograph, frozen in space and time and unable to capture the shifting characteristics of its changing territories. A truer picture would include a great deal of vitality and change, if for no other reason than that behavioral and social scientists, like all scientists, are committed as a matter of principle to open empirical investigation and to the revision or rejection of concepts and theories not supported by empirical demonstration. We focus on four illustrations of this vitality and change: (1) specialization within disciplines; (2) the improvement of data; (3) shifts in conceptual and theoretical focus; and (4) interdisciplinary ferment.

SPECIALIZATION

Each of the behavioral and social sciences, like other sciences, continually experiences internal specialization. As we noted in Chapter 1, new specialties arise as a consequence of advances in knowledge. Others develop around methodological innovations: Econometrics and survey analysis are examples. Still others develop around specific theoretical perspectives: Institutional economics, Freudian psychology, and different varieties of structuralism in psychology, anthropology, and sociology are illustrations. In addition, new specialties arise in response to the appearance of new social phenomena and new social problems that command the attention of behavioral and social scientists. The sociology of unemployment was developed and consolidated in the 1930s; the social psychology of propaganda was largely a child of World War II; and specialties like the sociology of leisure and the sociology of sports have developed as investigators began to investigate phenomena that had become important enough to be problematic.

IMPROVEMENT OF DATA

A great deal of scientific activity is concerned with the development of techniques for careful observation, accurate description, and precise measurement. As we note later, the social and behavioral sciences have made dramatic progress on this front in recent times. It might even be argued that the improvement of data represents the major area of advance. To mention only a few examples: It is now possible to describe the distribution of traits, attitudes, and behaviors in the population as a whole through the use of sample surveys; to monitor trends in the state of the economy and comparisons between economic systems through the use of national accounts and economic indicators; to analyze the behavior of newborn infants through visual preference techniques; and to assess the cognitive performance of individuals and populations through the use of standardized tests. The data generated by these means not only provide more accurate information about ourselves and our society but also facilitate the formulation and testing of more complex and sophisticated hypotheses about human behavior and social organizations than were previously possible.

Recent advances in demographic estimation techniques provide a striking example of the utility of improved measurement (for a review see the paper by Menken and Trussell in Part II). In the course of the last century, mathematical demographers have been able to work out detailed relationships between fertility rates, mortality rates, and the age structure of populations, particularly through the development of stable population theory. These relations have proved useful in projecting the future structure of populations, wherever sufficiently reliable data have been available. However, in developing nations, where the need for such information is perhaps most acute, data have been incomplete and inaccurate; work by Coale and Brass (Brass et al., 1968; United Nations Department of Economic and Social Affairs, 1967) and subsequent refinements (Hill et al., 1981) have made it possible to partly overcome this deficit by making use of known relationships among demographic variables to provide estimates from incomplete data. A project of the Committee on Population and Demography of the National Research Council is exploiting these techniques to develop reliable estimates of the demographic structures of a number of developing nations—estimates that would have been impossible not many years ago (Lapham, 1978).

As in the physical and biological sciences, the history of the social and behavioral sciences has been one of constant interaction between improvements in measurement and improvements in theory. For example, the development of national economic indictors by Kuznets (1941) in the 1930s made possible the systematic study of economic development, by providing a theoretically based and standardized metric of economic outcomes and economic growth. As is typically the case, the pioneering work of Kuznets did not solve for all time the problem of output and income measurements. His advances paved the way for further research and still further findings. To illustrate, journalists often conclude from the economic almanac of the World Bank that the United States has been surpassed in per-capita real gross national product by such countries as Switzerland, Sweden, and West Germany. This impression comes from translating Swiss francs, Swedish crowns, and German marks into dollars using official foreign exchange rates. When the United Nations and the World Bank sponsored a study to survey what prices people actually pay in spending their various incomes (Kravis et al., 1975), the errors in these impressions were made clear. U.S. per-capita income still surpasses in real terms that of Canada, Switzerland, Sweden, and West Germany. In this case, ongoing research into the economic theory of index numbers by regions, combined with expensive and time-consuming data gathering on actual local prices and incomes, is producing new insights and understanding of people's economic welfare.

SHIFTS IN CONCEPTUAL AND THEORETICAL FOCUS

The behavioral and social sciences, like other sciences, are characterized by dramatic cycles of conceptual innovation, the modification of old perspectives, and the consideration of new problems on the basis of new perspectives. Two examples illustrate this kind of cycle.

First, in classical economics, markets were regarded as peopled with a number of economic actors (e.g., households, firms) who produced, exchanged, and consumed goods and services according to the laws of supply and demand. Classical economists typically made a number of simplifying assumptions: that all economic actors had full knowledge of market conditions, that no economic actor had the power singly to influence output or prices, and that all economic actors would behave according to some kind of rational market calculus. Market processes were the direct objects of study, and the phenomena that were built into the assumptions were not objects for study, but remained unexamined givens.

In the subsequent history of economic thought, many of the advances of knowledge came not only from refining economic analysis in the context of these givens but also from challenging their status—that is, regarding the givens as subject to variability and studying them directly as influences on economic processes. Modern economic developments dealing with behavior under conditions of risk and uncertainty were built on modifications and reformulations of the assumption of perfect knowledge of market conditions. The development of theories of imperfect competition challenged the assumption that firms do not have the power to influence prices or output, assumed that in fact they did, and generated solutions or outcomes of market processes that were not possible under classical assumptions. Finally, Keynes (1936) altered the classical assumption that modern economies have an inherent tendency toward full employment and would adjust quickly to correct disturbances that resulted in unemployment. Keynes foresaw the possibility of chronic unemployment as an equilibrium position (that is, as the condition toward which an economy might tend to move), which was difficult to envision under classical assumptions. In these examples the dynamic is one of questioning what was previously taken as economic reality and reformulating the nature of economic processes—that is, making them a special case of some larger family of processes or making them contingent on a more inclusive order of determinants than had previously been taken into account. The paper by Heckman and Michael (in Part II) gives an account of recent conceptual development in the area of labor economics.

The second example concerns explanations of crime. In the late 19th and early 20th centuries, the dominant explanations of crime were built on the assumption that its main determinants lay in the biological realm, and various efforts were made to identify characteristic physical traits or body types associated with criminal behavior. While these explanations were crude and hardly qualify as theory in any formal sense, they nonetheless contained the assumption that psychological or temperamental features of criminal behavior were either altogether unimportant or derivative from more fundamental biological determinants; moreover, the social contexts of crime were altogether unexamined. Crime was thought to be determined objectively by biological factors.

Subsequent developments in the study of crime have challenged this assumption. One new branch of theory and investigation, stimulated mainly by the psychoanalytic perspective, has regarded crime as the "acting out" of deep psychological conflicts; for example, in one formulation, criminality derives from a sense of guilt. Other approaches have stressed social disorganization and social contradictions as generating crime; others have explained it as behavior learned in particular social environments. Still others have focused on the social determinants of how particular acts come to be defined as crimes, noting that a given act may or may not be regarded as criminal depending on the outcome of a political struggle. Drinking in public places, which was constitutionally banned at one point in our history, is a case in point, as is the current struggle over the legality of abortion. Some very recent efforts have acknowledged the importance of all three levels—

biological, psychological, and social—and have begun the attempt to construct interactive models incorporating a variety of these kinds of variables.

These cycles of reformulation may find their origins at the level of theoretical discourse, when theorists attempt to challenge the underpinnings of some explanation and revise it by changing its assumptions; or the appearance of empirical anomalies that cannot be accounted for under accepted theories may demand new explanations. Whatever their origins, these cycles leave in their wake an array of competitive schools or approaches. In an ideal scientific world, the alternative approaches would be assessed, and accepted or rejected accordingly, according to their capacity to account for observed phenomena and generate new hypotheses. The world is not so perfect, however; existing approaches do not disappear when new ones appear, or even when they are shown to be superior. Indeed, sometimes they need not, since existing approaches may address a different range of problems. In any event, proponents of the old and new approaches may not agree on the criteria for a decisive, once-and-for-all evaluation of one theory over another. Again, these tendencies characterize all scientific fields to some extent.

INTERDISCIPLINARY FERMENT

The continuous development of areas of inquiry also arises as a kind of synthetic fusion of ideas and investigations around problems that are not unambiguously assignable to one discipline but draw on the resources of many. We mention four instances of these kinds of interdisciplinary endeavors.

The first is an interest in the human life-span as a focus of study. A relatively new but vital focus of scientific inquiry, this area has drawn contributions from developmental psychologists, psychoanalysts, sociologists, and demographic historians as well as some physiologists and biologists. An important insight stemming from this perspective is that developmental change occurs over the entire course of life rather than being restricted to the childhood years; by the same token, behavior and personality remain malleable throughout life. This discovery has extremely important policy implications for the redesign of programs and facilities for the aged. A more detailed discussion of these developments is presented in the paper by Featherman (in Part II).

The second example is the development of an area of inquiry known as social choice. Peopled mainly by economists and political scientists but including some others as well, this special area involves the study of determinants, dynamics, and outcomes of processes by which societies make decisions about policies affecting their members; it includes as well the study of criteria for evaluating these processes. This area is described in more detail in Chapter 3.

The third example concerns the great volume of research that goes under the heading of comparative international research, involving the study of regions of the world (such as Southeast Asia), the study of transnational institutions (such as corporations and banks), and the study of international economic, political, and social systems. Built on no single behavioral or social science discipline, these lines of inquiry are inherently interdisciplinary, involving economists, geographers, political scientists, social anthropologists, sociologists, and historians as well as scholars from the humanistic disciplines, and represent one of the main areas of close and active collaboration between American and foreign social scientists.

A final example is what has come in the last two decades to be called policy studies. Policy analysis combines the intellectual efforts of political scientists, geographers, economists, sociologists, and statisticians. Often organized in special schools or programs within universities, researchers in this area investigate the conditions that give rise to particular public policies, evaluate how well they achieve their objectives, and study the unanticipated consequences of policy interventions.

As these kinds of interdisciplinary efforts evolve, participants communicate informally with one another, hold meetings, develop small professional associations, and perhaps develop specialized publications such as newsletters or journals.

A FINAL WORD

Taking into consideration the dynamics of specialization, the development of data, theoretical shifts, and interdisciplinary activity—and the interactions of all of these with one another—the behavioral and social sciences resemble not so much a map as a kaleidoscope, with continuous growth, shifting boundaries, and new emphases and highlights.

EXPLANATORY MODES AND METHODS IN THE BEHAVIORAL AND SOCIAL SCIENCES

As the foregoing has suggested, the behavioral and social sciences are highly diverse, ranging from the study of meaning to the study of human fossils. Nonetheless, it is possible to identify a few central themes that characterize the aims, the modes of explanation, and the methods of most of these disciplines.

First, with respect to aims there are two largely competitive visions, which gives some credence to the notion postulated by C. P. Snow that the social and behavioral sciences are intermediate between the two cultures of science and the humanities. The dominant vision is shared with the biological and physical sciences: The goal of scientific inquiry is the cumulative development of empirically verified generalizations about the conditions under which events or phenomena occur and about how they are organized and interrelated. Attempts to identify the general principles by which organisms learn, to specify the conditions under which prices rise and fall, and to account for the tendency of social classes to reproduce themselves are examples of this general approach, in which the aims of research in the social and behavioral sciences are taken to be no different from those of any other science. The fact that many generalizations or laws in the behavioral and social sciences are probabilistic rather than deterministic, tendencies rather than absolutes, allies these disciplines with much of biology and with areas of physical science as diverse as quantum mechanics and meteorology and distinguishes them from the deterministic approaches of 19th-century physics and chemistry.

Generalization of any sort requires abstraction. Much research in the behavioral and social sciences involves the systematic study of a limited number of phenomena—variables—abstracted from the context in which they are embedded. Formal demography, for example, largely involves the working out of the interrelations among four variables—birth rates, death rates, age, and sex—to determine their consequences for the size, growth, and distribution of populations (see the paper by Menken and Trussell in Part II). Often such abstraction is required to discern the underlying connections between phenomena of interest, which tend to be obscured by the additional influence of other factors when studied in context. For example, just as assertions about the effect of atmospheric pressure on the boiling point of water are in fact assertions about H_2O and not about Potomac River water or Pacific Ocean water, which contain much more besides H_2O, assertions about the responsiveness of prices to changes in supply and demand are abstractions from what actually happens to the price of a particular good being sold at a particular time in a particular market.

The need to simplify and abstract behavior in the interest of discovering general laws is seen by some social and behavioral scientists (indeed, a sizable fraction in several of these disciplines) as producing results that do not greatly enhance our understanding of the human condition. These scholars have an alternative vision. For them, human behavior and social arrangements are regarded as arising from particular concrete historical circumstances and hence are appropriately studied in the context of these circumstances. The goal of research for these scholars thus is not generalization—many would question whether the sort of generalization that characterizes the physical and biological sciences is possible—but *interpretation*. Their emphasis is on understanding what is distinctive rather than what is general. For example, someone working in this tradition would be less interested in noting the analogies between Japanese and European feudalism and asking why it is that similar social forms arose in such widely disparate settings than in working out the specifics of the relationships between lord and vassal in the Japanese or European context. One social scientist has contrasted the two approaches as a "laws-and-instances ideal of explanation" and a "cases-and-interpretations one" (Geertz, 1980:165). Both approaches must be encompassed in a complete understanding of the nature of research in the social and behavioral sciences.

Crosscutting this distinction are differences among and within the behavioral and social sciences with respect to both the types of data used and the methods of analysis employed. Like astronomy and geology, most of the behavioral and social sciences are observational rather than experimental disciplines. Only in a few of these fields does experimentation play an important role. Although relying mainly on nonexperimental data, many of these fields are highly quantitative. Relatively elaborate statistical procedures have been developed to approximate as closely as possible by statistical adjustments the kind of control of extraneous factors possible in experimental procedures.

These distinctions lead naturally to the identification of three distinctive modes of analysis: experimentation, statistical control, and statistically uncontrolled observation. As with our catalogue of disciplines, however, these categories permit only a crude summary of. the range and variety of analytic procedures used in the behavioral and social sciences. The three modes of analysis form a framework for the remainder of the discussion in this chapter.

EXPERIMENTATION

In some areas of behavioral and social research, true experimentation is possible. Experiments are studies in which the objects of study are divided into categories and the categories are subjected to different treatments. If differential effects are observed, they are presumed to be due to the difference in treatments. In the behavioral and social sciences, experiments typically are conducted by assigning individuals randomly to groups and then subjecting the groups to different treatments. The necessity for random assignment is due to the fact that individuals ordinarily differ in ways other than those being manipulated in the experiment, and these differences may affect the outcomes. By randomizing the assignment of individuals to different treatments, these extraneous effects are averaged out, which makes it possible to infer, within known limits of error, that whatever post-treatment differences between groups are observed were *caused* by the treatment.

For example, in a study of the effect of suggestion on memory, Loftus (1975) showed subjects a brief videotape of an automobile accident, then asked them questions about it. For half the subjects, one of the questions was: "How fast was the white sports car going while traveling along the country road?" For the other half, a similar question was: "How fast was the white sports car going when it passed the barn while traveling along the country road?" In fact, there was no barn in the film. Yet when questioned again about the accident a week later, more than 17 percent of those exposed to the false information about a barn answered "yes" to the question: "Did you see a barn?" In contrast, only about 3 percent of the other subjects answered "yes" to the same question. Apparently, the assumption of the existence of a barn during the initial questioning caused many subjects to incorporate the nonexistent barn into their recollection of the event. Moreover, a subsequent experiment showed that simply asking people whether they had seen a barn—a question to which they usually answered "no"—was enough to increase the likelihood that they would later incorporate a barn into their memories of the accident. Research of this kind has important implications for eyewitness testimony. In criminal and civil trials, jurors tend to believe the testimony of eyewitnesses. Yet, as this and similar experiments show, such testimony can be faulty.

While most experimental work in the behavioral and social sciences is done in psychology, a particularly interesting set of experimental studies was carried out by economists and sociologists to investigate the effect of federal subsidies to low-income families (negative income tax) on the incentive to seek paid employment. Such experiments were carried out at several sites: some towns in New Jersey; Seattle, Washington; Denver, Colorado; Gary, Indiana; and a number of rural areas. In the New Jersey experiment (Kershaw and Fair, 1976-1977) the interest was in testing how families would respond to varying levels of income subsidy and various rates of "taxation" (that is, partial reduction in the subsidy for people who earn income on their own). The issue was whether people would lose their incentive to work because they were being supported by public funds. This particular experiment included only families with male heads who were able to work. A sample of about 1,300 low-income families was selected and subsidized at various rates for a three-year period. The main finding of this research, which has occasioned some lively debate (Rossi and Lyall, 1976), is that income subsidies do not appear to reduce incentives to work.

STATISTICAL CONTROL

Often in the behavioral and social sciences, as in the clinical areas of medical research, true experimentation is not possible. Both ethical and practical considerations severely limit the kinds of experiments that can be done using human subjects. In addition, many events of interest to social scientists are simply not experimentally manipulable. The propensity for in-group solidarity to increase in wartime, for example, is not something that can be experimentally confirmed; nor can the proposition that social stratification is more pronounced in sedentary agricultural societies than in hunter-gatherer societies.

To overcome this limitation, a variety of statistical procedures have been devised to simulate experimental conditions by holding constant or controlling those variables that are thought to influence a particular outcome but are not of interest to the investigator, and to investigate the net contribution of each of several variables to a given outcome. Such procedures are sometimes simple and straightforward but can often become quite complex.

A common starting point in social and behavioral research is the observation that two variables are *associated*—that is, that individuals in a population tend to have similar values on both variables (or dissimilar values, in which case we speak of negative association). For example, income and education are associated, because those with high education tend also to have high income; gender and earnings are associated, because men tend to have higher earnings than women. Over time the homicide rate and the suicide rate of a population are negatively associated, because one tends to rise as the other falls.

Association alone does not indicate a causal relationship. The association between two variables may be the product of a third variable that has determined the value of both, so that their association indicates only a common cause. An example, made famous by its presentation to many generations of social science students, is the observation that babies are associated with storks—that is, areas with lots of storks tend to have high birth rates. From this observation, one would not want to conclude that storks bring babies, at least not without first statistically controlling for size of place in order to test the hypothesis that the observed association arises because rural areas tend to have both high birth rates and large stork populations.

This example illustrates both the logic and the limitation of statistical controls. If it turned out that within areas (rural and urban) there was no relationship between stork density and birth rates, we could readily conclude that the observed association between babies and storks was due to their common cause, the different characters of rural and urban places. But suppose it turned out that urban areas with many storks and rural areas with many storks both had higher birth rates than the corresponding areas with few storks. Could we then conclude that storks bring babies? No, because still other factors might be involved. Perhaps, due to accidents of geography and history, storks tend to be found in Catholic areas (this is a European example). Catholics tend to have higher birth rates than Protestants for reasons that have nothing to do with storks. So possibly it is religion, not storks, that affects the birth rate. Or possibly it is something associated with religion to some degree, like income, education, or occupation, that is the major operative force. The point is that, in contrast to experiments, in nonexperimental work one can never be sure that all of the relevant factors have been controlled. That is a major limitation of the approach.

In an effort to overcome this limitation, social and behavioral scientists and statisticians have developed a powerful array of mathematical and statistical procedures designed to permit inferences about the behavior and interrelations of sets of variables connected to each other in complex ways. Multiple regression analysis and its extensions and elaborations have become standard tools in economics and sociology and are widely used in most of the other behavioral and social sciences as well (Van de Geer, 1971). Much work has gone into the development of formal models, in which the relations among variables are expressed in terms of mathematical equations. A relatively simple example of such a model is described in Chapter 3 in the discussion of the analysis of status attainment. Much more complex models, some involving hundreds of variables, have been developed for the purpose of economic forecasting; such models are discussed in Chapter 4.

These developments have gone hand in hand with the development of sampling procedures that permit inferences to be made about large populations on the basis of information obtained from relatively small samples. Since the data used in much social and behavioral research are drawn from people, organizations, and other relatively heterogeneous populations, the researcher is not free to assume that one individual is like every other. One bacterium may be much like another of the same kind, but one middle-aged male professor probably is not enough like another that they can be assumed to be interchangeable. Given this, a researcher interested in the behavior of middle-aged male professors must either collect data on all of them or on a sample of them drawn in such a way that it can be assumed, within known limits of error, to represent all of them. The sample survey, discussed in Chapter 4, is an important technique for accomplishing this, but behavioral and social scientists use sampling procedures to collect other sorts of data as well. See the paper by Tanur (in Part II) for an extended discussion of this topic.

STATISTICALLY UNCONTROLLED OBSERVATION

There are many research problems in the behavioral and social sciences for which it is not possible, practical, or desirable to collect sample data or to attempt statistical controls. Such problems cover a broad range, from the analysis of many (although not all) kinds of historical data to the interpretation of cultures. Descriptions of myths or rituals often fall into this category, gaining significance from the interweaving of recounted or enacted symbols with ongoing social relationships. So do processes of change that may be adequately known only from a single well-documented occurrence but that still sustain a kind of interpretative generalization if stress is placed on the contextural setting of the institutions, beliefs, and behavior with which they are associated. Comparative studies also can be carried out on this basis; comparisons between a limited number of concrete cases may not permit or warrant statistical analysis but sometimes can be abstracted into informative contrasts of structure and function. Another example of this kind of study is the detailed clinical investigation of individuals with complex or unusual personality disorders. Such studies provide the richest kinds of primary data, capture the texture of social life firsthand, and often are valuable as a means of generating hypotheses. Moreover, there is often no substitute for a richly descriptive approach that takes full command of masses of heterogeneous and confusing data if one wishes to sort out and assess the significance of behavioral codes that prevail in a particular society or culture.

Finally, the search for counterexamples through what is essentially uncontrolled observation can have an important influence on hypotheses about universals. For example, it was once widely assumed that the nuclear family (mother, father, and children) was a fundamental unit in all societies. Contrary cases in the ethnographic literature then were adduced and intensively debated. Was it useful or sufficient, the challenge ran, to base a claim for the family's universality on a definition of it in purely formal terms? A functional approach, which seemed in many respects more helpful, led to a further proliferation of possibilities. Should the family be thought of as the primary locus for the socialization of children? Must we think of it as a coresidential unit? Should families embody common economic functions to be recognized as such? Or, at a minimum, is the family merely a procreational unit? What emerges from continuing discussions along these lines, at least at this writing, is neither a reaffirmed universal rule nor an unequivocal refutation of one. Instead, a social institution has taken on a richer texture when viewed from opposing as well as complementary perspectives. Variant cases have shed light on the complexity and adaptability of what is undeniably a basic social feature. We less often test a hypothesis like this than we come to understand its potential range of applications and ambiguities. Contrary cases, in a word, need not be so much negative as additive.

3

Knowledge from the Behavioral and Social Sciences: Examples

It is illuminating to compare our understanding of the nature of human behavior and social organization with beliefs held just a few decades or even a few years ago. In almost every area of the behavioral and social sciences, widely accepted understandings have been transformed by ongoing research.

To illustrate the breadth and variety of basic research in the social and behavioral sciences, this chapter presents a set of vignettes briefly describing developments in a few areas of research. The vast range and variety of research in the behavioral and social sciences makes a comprehensive survey of such efforts impossible in a report of this kind. The committee has found it possible to proceed only by a process of heroic selection of a few examples in which there has been substantial advancement of understanding in the recent past. We imagine that different choices would have been made by another similarly constituted group, but the necessity for choice could not have been avoided. Even with regard to areas of research in the social and behavioral sciences in which rapid progress is occurring, the topics chosen for inclusion are but a small fraction. They are intended to provide a sense of the variety of activity in these disciplines, in sufficient detail to suggest the richness of discovery sometimes attending it. Some but not all of these topics are developed more fully in the papers that accompany this report.

These vignettes serve also to illustrate three fundamental features of basic research. First, it is often interdisciplinary; second, substantive advances often depend on improvements in measurement procedures and research

33

strategies; and third, research intended purely to improve understanding often leads to practical applications. This last point is merely touched on here, since it is the main topic of the next chapter.

As these vignettes illustrate, there is a great deal of cross-fertilization between fields, both within and beyond the behavioral and social sciences, with respect to theories, concepts, and methods. The study of primate evolution, for example, has profited enormously from the development of biochemical methods for assessing species similarity. Similarly, the study of social stratification was transformed through the use of statistical procedures first developed for use in population genetics and, in a somewhat independent line of development, elaborated by econometricians. The new field of cognitive science has drawn from the insights of linguists, computer scientists, and logicians as well as psychologists. And theorists in anthropology, sociology, and political science who characterize their respective domains as systems have, over the decades, borrowed organismic and other models from the biological sciences. Statistical procedures for the analysis of events occurring over time (time series), developed by statisticians working on problems in the social sciences, have been adapted for use in weather and climate prediction, statistical astronomy, and epidemiological studies. The propensity for disciplines to borrow from one another should serve to remind us of the arbitrary nature of the labels *physical*, *biological*, *behavioral*, and *social* science. Is the study of human origins a biological or a social science? Its methods are now largely drawn from the physical and biochemical sciences, while its explanations of human evolution depend heavily on ideas about the nature of social interaction. Similarly, interpretation of the fossil record depends in part on an analysis of the implements and cultural debris found near fossil remains, while the construction of a chronological framework would often be impossible without the dating methods derived from the physical sciences.

The vignettes are arranged deliberately in no particular sequence to emphasize that they cannot be fully representative of the totality of work within particular disciplines; they should be taken in their entirety as an attempt to convey the variety of research activity encompassed by the behavioral and social sciences.

VOTING

The centrality that democratic theory assigns to elections and therefore to the act of voting has naturally promoted studies of voting in American political science and sociology. The essential questions of basic research on voting are easy to state, although difficult to answer: first, at the individual level, how citizens decide whether to vote and who to vote for; and, second, how individual votes are aggregated to make collective decisions (a question that has close ties with the theory of social choice, discussed below). Modern voting research began about 50 years ago with the collection of the first survey data on how individual voters made their decisions. It was given a strong boost after World War II by the failure of commercial polling houses to predict accurately the outcome of the 1948 presidential election. Subsequently it has become an extremely vigorous area, supported by an ongoing series of national election surveys conducted by the Survey Research Center of the University of Michigan.

The history of this topic has been one of formulation and testing of successively more complex (and more realistic) models of voting behavior Early research by Lazarsfeld and his colleagues (1944) revealed that actual voting behavior runs counter to widely held beliefs about how voters decide among candidates—particularly to the notion that the typical voter makes a rational decision based on careful consideration of the candidates' records and stated positions on issues. These investigators started their research with the idea that voters behaved somewhat like consumers exposed to advertising campaigns: Over the course of the campaign, voters would be exposed to competing claims by the candidates, and they would weigh these claims to arrive at a final voting decision in much the same way as consumers were presumed to digest the competing claims of advertisers to arrive at a decision about a brand to purchase. To capture the process of decision making, they designed a panel survey, in which the same voters were interviewed on a monthly basis, beginning in May 1940, well before the presidential campaign began, and continuing through the election in November. As it turned out, their fundamental premise was erroneous: Almost all voters had made their decision in May, before they even knew who the candidates would be. That is, they voted a party preference, rather than for a particular candidate. Less than 10 percent of the panel changed their preference during the campaign, and these turned out to be the least sophisticated voters, who were least involved in the election; their willingness to change preference was due to indifference rather than a careful consideration of the alternatives.

These unanticipated results fundamentally altered the conception of voting behavior and led to the investigation of important new questions: What does account for swings in the popular vote from one election to the next? Under what circumstances do such shifts lead to a fundamental realignment of the electorate?

A series of biennial surveys of national elections initiated at the University of Michigan in the 1950s plus a series of long-term historical studies provided answers to these questions: While most voters simply follow a party preference, under circumstances of special stress or special attraction to the candidate of the opposing party, they may engage in short-term defection. Voters recognize their defection as such and ordinarily return to their original party in the next election. However, occasionally there are "critical" or "realigning" elections, in which major shifts take place in long-term party alignments. The last definitively critical election period was that of the 1932-1934 presidential and congressional elections; it is still too early to decide whether the 1980 presidential election signaled a new realignment.

The Michigan studies and others also led to the solution of a number of other puzzles regarding voting behavior. Why does the party occupying the White House invariably lose congressional seats in off-year elections? It turns out to be a matter of who votes. In presidential election years the voter turnout is higher, drawing people with unstable voting preferences as well as party regulars, and the party that gets these swing votes captures the White House. But in off-year congressional elections only party regulars bother to vote, pulling the vote closer to the long-term equilibrium. Why do presidential and other candidates often seem to take very similar positions near the center of the ideological spectrum? It can be shown that by taking a position as close to the center as possible candidates will maximize the number of votes they get. This result also accounts for the nonideological character of much voting—there is not much room for decision making on the basis of the issues if very little distinguishes the candidates—and has led to a much more sophisticated version of the rational voter model. In this model the emphasis is on explaining the behavior of the small fraction of voters in any election for whom real choices are available; it thereby focuses on explaining shifts in the vote from election to election rather than on explaining the total vote in each election. Such shifts turn out to be largely a matter of rational responses to candidates' positions on issues perceived to be important by voters.

Subsequent research has expanded in three directions. First, there has been an increase in the range of influences implicated in the voting process, and current models encompass a wide range of influences: voter characteristics, such as personality-rooted motivations, learned social and political attitudes, role-dependent perceptions and expectations, interpersonal relations and pressures, and group-linked and institutional constraints; self-presentations and behaviors of candidates in campaigns; the behavior of the mass media; the influence of campaign finances and the activities of party organizations and interest groups; the impact of long-term social and economic conditions; and the facilities and impediments of the electoral mechanism itself.

Second, there has been a very substantial export of the Michigan surveys to other countries, and data are now beginning to accumulate that will permit an assessment of whether the voting behavior observed in the United States is characteristic of industrialized democracies in general. The accumulation of data on past elections also permits us to see how stable voting behavior has been in the United States over a period of nearly 30 years. A preliminary assessment is that party identification is lessening and voters are becoming more issue-oriented but that these trends are relatively weak.

Third, there has been increased attention to other parts of the voting system, apart from decision making by individual voters, with particular emphasis on strategies adopted by candidates and the legislative behavior of elected representatives. These and other topics are reviewed in more detail in the paper on voting by Converse et al. (in Part II).

HISTORY OF THE FAMILY

As the result of efforts by social scientists in many disciplines who have vigorously explored data from numerous sources with the aid of multivariate statistical procedures, it is now possible to describe modern family life with a fair integration of the particulars of internal family practices, ethnic, class, and national cultural settings, and the location of these styles of life within vast historical and world trends. As yet no theories predict or explain such wide ranges of human behavior, but we can now observe and judge family and population problems with a much higher degree of precision than was possible 30 years ago. The paper by Featherman (in Part II) illustrates the approach of life-span research to this topic.

It is fitting that American researchers should date the origins of their studies of the family with the publication in 1798 of Malthus's *Essay on the Principle of Population*, since the Reverend Malthus based his reasoning on the first population census of the United States. To Malthus and those who followed him for the next century and a half, the family was the product of historical events, not the maker of history in its own right.

Such an outlook had almost been forced on them. Those were the years of the population explosion of the Atlantic world, of vast international and transoceanic migrations, of crop failures and famines, of sudden epidemics of cholera, typhus, and yellow fever, of rapid industrialization, and of the sudden appearance of new cities and towns and giant new metropolises. In such a climate of social transformations, it is no wonder that demographers and historians viewed modern families as the product of massive environmental shifts, and no wonder, either, that they focused particularly on the most common new type—the nuclear family of husband, wife, and a few children.

By the early decades of the 20th century, through careful statistical work, social scientists had charted the major paths of European and Atlantic migration, mapped the spread of urbanization and industrialization (Weber, 1899), and established an overall historical sequence that seemed to explain the flourishing of the small nuclear family in urban industrialized societies.

At this point in the progress of family scholarship, the anomalies grew in importance. The French population did not migrate overseas as readily as other Europeans, and the French rural population had been sharply limiting its family size for decades before any mechanized factories or industrial towns appeared. The fertility of the Irish population never recovered from the potato famines of the 1840s. In the United States the birth rate had fallen steadily with every census from 1800 on, despite ample harvests and abundant land (it did not begin to rise until 1950). After World War I European populations did not replace their losses either as fast as previously or as fast as their governments urged them to. Clearly there was a latitude to family decision making about marriage, births, and employment that far exceeded the Malthusian cycles of food and famine or the later model of demographic transition from premodern culture to urban industrialized culture. The desire to improve the quality of family and demographic history gained urgency after World War II, when populations of non-European nations exploded and the question arose as to whether the European experience with the flourishing of the small nuclear family would repeat itself throughout the modern world.

Today's answer to this postwar question is a complicated one, because we have learned that the European experience compounded many more ingredients than formerly were recognized. The first step in recognizing this complexity began with a careful reexamination of time series data on American and European families, a process facilitated by the introduction of the computer and the improvement of demographic estimation techniques (which are described in the paper by Menken and Trussell in Part II).

At the same time the question of non-European economic development spurred another reexamination of American history. In this case economists concerned with the relationships among capital formation, migration, and population growth began to tabulate these variables on a regional basis, comparing one aspect of the nation's experience with others. In this research the family and its aggregated decisions to move, to marry, and to have children appeared as an active force in history, not merely as an outcome of other forces (Kuznets and Thomas, 1957-1964).

From quite another direction sociologists began to question the proposition that the modern nuclear family had taken its form to meet the demands of the modern factory. Perhaps, they reasoned, the factory itself, in some of its history and in some of its current particulars of hours, work rules, and employment policies, reflects the preferences of families. And so it turned out. A core institution of industrialization thus proved to be part of a complex interaction among large and small social forces (Smelser, 1959; Hareven, 1975; Hirsch, 1978; Hershberg, 1981).

Freudian psychology provided yet another impetus for family and demographic study. The Freudians' stress on the importance of childrearing practices (E. Erikson, 1950) encouraged the interests of anthropologists, who in turn speculated that perhaps alternative family practices might have major consequences for modern ethnic, class, and even national cultures. This anthropological work in turn stimulated historians, who began careful studies of villages in which the family histories of entire settlements were undertaken. The anthropological example was further imitated in that attention was focused on the interrelations among all the local institutions—the religion, economy, and technology. As might be expected, villages proved to be far from uniform, and, more surprising, they revealed many modern character-istics, even in the Middle Ages—for example, nuclear families and high rates of geographic mobility. Centered in a group at Cambridge University in England, this historical work on villages and families soon generated fresh interpretations of European and American social and family history (Laslett, 1965, 1969; Wrigley, 1969; Grevern, 1970).

As a result of the rapid accumulation of such a variety of studies, the conception of the family shifted from that of a mere mechanical respondent to that of an interacting human institution that both molds and is molded by society and history.

No overarching theoretical synthesis has yet resulted. Social scientists cannot yet link in any causal statement all the important variables of family life, which range from courtship practices and child care to industrialization and urbanization. But the cumulation of recent research does permit us to be much more specific about what must be attended to in order to describe or discuss the present or past circumstances of a nation's population.

We have learned that family practices with respect to marriage, children, employment, property, and extended kin are culturally specific. Whether we are observing the impact of a factory's coming to a village or of a countryman's moving to the city, we know to watch for a range of possible responses. Sometimes the responses of families are communitarian and involve extensive connections with churches, clubs, and labor unions; other families at other times respond to change by elaborating their kin networks; others pursue highly individualistic education and property-oriented responses; still others try to carry on as if no changes had taken place around them (Barton, 1975). Furthermore, we have learned that modern urbanized populations conduct their family life according to class subcultures, and, to make matters more complicated, each of these class subcultures is subject to trends of fashion in family goals and family behavior. For example, the current middle-class American pattern of attentive and permissive childrearing became a fashion among that class in the late 19th century. How long the fashion will flourish is unpredictable, but it is useful to notice that a similar fashion, among a similar class, prevailed in England from the late 17th to the early 19th century, when it was replaced by a more repressive mode. All the latest summary work in family history stresses the class structure and class waves of family fashions, and this work contends that the waves of fashion do not correspond to economic or political cycles (Stone, 1977).

BEHAVIOR AND HEALTH

As the effects of psychosocial and behavioral variables on biological processes have come to be recognized, the social and behavioral sciences have made increasingly important contributions to the understanding of problems of physical health. Many medical problems, including heart disease and cancer, appear to be influenced by behavioral and social variables, such as habits of living (e.g., smoking, diet, alcohol, exercise), and by what has been termed psychosocial stress. The processes linking behavior to physical illness are of three types: (1) direct alterations in tissue function through the brain's influence on hormone production and other physiological responses to psychosocial stimuli, particularly stress; (2) health-impairing habits and life-styles, such as smoking, heavy drinking, lack of exercise, poor diet, and poor hygienic practices; and (3) reactions to illness, including minimization of the significance of symptoms, delay in seeking medical care, and failure to comply with treatment and rehabilitation regimens. These processes are reviewed in greater detail in the paper by Krantz et al. (in Part II).

DIRECT PSYCHOPHYSIOLOGICAL EFFECTS

In the first category are bodily changes that occur under conditions of stress in the absence of external agents such as cigarette smoke or high-cholesterol food. Stress has been defined as a nonspecific response of the body to external demands that are placed on it (Selye, 1956); in a more psychological sense, stress refers to a perceived imbalance between the demands imposed on an individual and his or her felt ability to cope with them (Cox, 1978). Examples of stress-inducing stimuli are work pressures, marital disruption, and geographical mobility.

Physiological responses to stress include neural and endocrine activity, which in turn can influence a wide range of bodily processes, including metabolic rate, cardiovascular and autonomic nervous system functioning, and immune reactions (Mason, 1971; Levi, 1979). Short-term stress responses include hormonal and cardiovascular reactions (e.g., increased heart rate, higher blood pressure), which may precipitate clinical disorders (e.g., stroke, cardiac instabilities, and pain symptoms) in predisposed individuals. If the stressful stimuli are pronounced, prolonged, or repetitive, the result may be chronic dysfunction in one or more systems (e.g, the gastrointestinal or cardiovascular systems).

Research on psychosocial variables related to the pathogenesis of cardio-vascular disorders provides a good example of direct psychophysiological effects in the etiology of disease. Perhaps the most thoroughly investigated psychosocial risk factor for coronary heart disease is what is called the type A behavior pattern (Rosenman and Friedman, 1974). Type A personalities are characterized by extreme competitiveness and striving for achievement, a strong sense of time urgency and impatience, hostility, and aggressiveness. Personalities that do not exhibit this syndrome of traits are designated type B. Although several studies have documented an association between type A behavior and coronary heart disease, the best evidence comes from the Western Collaborative Group Study (Rosenman et al., 1975), in which more than 3,000 initially healthy men, ages 39 to 59, were assessed on a comprehensive array of social, dietary, biochemical, clinical, and behavioral variables. A follow-up study after eight and a half years showed that subjects exhibiting type A behavior at the study's inception were about twice as likely as type B individuals to develop coronary heart disease. This differential in risk persisted when statistical procedures were used to control for the influence of other risk factors, such as cigarette smoking, serum cholesterol, and high blood pressure. In other words, these other factors do not account for the difference between type A and type B individuals in the probability of developing heart disease.

HEALTH-IMPAIRING HABITS AND LIFE-STYLES

Another way in which behavior leads to physical illness is the pursuit by some individuals of habits and styles of life that are damaging to health. Personal habits play a critical role in the development of many serious diseases. Cigarette smoking is probably the most salient behavior in this category, for it has been implicated as a risk factor in the three leading causes of death in the United States: coronary heart disease, cancer, and stroke. Poor diet, lack of exercise, excessive consumption of alcohol, and poor hygienic practices have also been linked to disease outcomes. These habits may be deeply rooted in cultural practices or initiated by social influences (e.g., smoking to obtain peer group approval). They may be maintained as part of an achievement-oriented life-style or by the interaction of biological and behavioral mechanisms of addiction. Therefore a major focus of research in behavioral medicine has been on the role of sociocultural systems, life-styles, and psychophysiological processes in the etiology and pathogenesis of chronic diseases. Considerable attention has also been directed toward the development of techniques to modify those behaviors that constitute risk factors for illnesses.

A particularly interesting example of the complex interplay between psychological and biological processes is the demonstration by Schacter et al. (1977) that heavy smokers adjust their smoking rate to keep the nicotine level in their body at a roughly constant level, so that the rate of smoking depends on the rate of nicotine excretion and breakdown by the body. The rate of nicotine excretion depends in part on the acid-base balance (pH) of the urine, which in turn can be altered by psychologial stress or anxiety. A physiologically mediated craving for cigarettes thus depends directly on the smoker's psychological state, explaining why smokers tend to light up a cigarette when they are nervous.

REACTIONS TO ILLNESS AND THE SICK ROLE

A third process through which behavior leads to physical illness is the practice of some individuals of minimizing the significance of symptoms, delaying in seeking medical care, or failing to comply with treatment and rehabilitation regimens. One prominent example is the sizable number of heart attack patients who procrastinate in seeking help, thereby endangering their chances of survival. Many other examples exist of circumstances in which people refuse to acknowledge that they are sick and hence do not do what is necessary to get well. These actions are representative of a larger area of study concerned with the way people react to the experience of organ dysfunction as well as to the experience of being in the role of a sick person. To succeed, medical therapies require that a patient follow his or her physician's advice, yet an extensive literature reports low rates of compliance with health and medical care regimens (Sackett and Haynes, 1976). Accordingly, there has been considerable research on social and psychological processes involved in patients' reactions to pain and illness, the decision to seek medical care, and compliance with medical treatments.

A good deal of attention has been given to isolating factors that influence or predict compliance (Sackett and Haynes, 1976; Becker, 1979). Contrary to the expectations of the medical profession, social and demographic characteristics such as age, sex, marital and socioeconomic status, and educational level turn out to have little relation to compliance; the most important influence on compliance is the quality of the doctor-patient interaction. Physicians who engender trust on the part of their patients and who explain the treatment regimen in comprehensible ways achieve much greater compliance than do others.

PRIMARY GROUPS IN LARGE-SCALE SOCIETY

One of the laments of modern life, promoted heavily in the rhetoric of the popular press, is that the scale of society is too large. Big cities, big government, big business, big schools have led to a depersonalization of relationships and the decline of the primary group—composed of family, friends, and neighbors—as the organizing basis of social life. As with all such generalizations, there is a grain of truth to this one. There no doubt has been a shift in the character of modern life, epitomized in such phrases as "mass society" and "the eclipse of community."

Yet, to paraphrase Mark Twain, rumors of the death of the primary group have proved greatly exaggerated. Social scientists working in different corners of society have repeatedly confirmed the hardiness and tenacity of the primary group, often in unlikely places. Consider the following: In the Chicago school of urban sociology, which developed mainly during the period of very rapid industrialization and urbanization in the first third of this century and which dominated sociology at that time, cities had come to be regarded as a kind of epitome of depersonalization if not outright disorganization of modern social life (Zorbaugh, 1929; Wirth, 1938). Careful empirical research has, however, corrected this view. One of the classic studies in sociology employing field observation, Whyte's *Street Corner Society* (1955), revealed the pervasiveness of men's friendship groups, which constituted the main source of social cohesiveness for men in the Italian-American slums of Boston. Years later, Elliot Liebow (1967) observed the same phenomenon among lower-class blacks in Washington, D.C., who, while experiencing the greatest fragility and instability of their work and family lives, fell back into neighborhood friendship groups for support, intimacy, and material help. Still more recent research by Carol Stack (1974) has refuted the stereotype of family disintegration among lower-class blacks, documenting the stability of kin-based networks of social support. Recent survey research in urban areas has shown a similar persistence of familial, friendship, and ethnic bases of integration for most people, although the "skid row" population and the urban elderly are major exceptions (Fischer, 1976). And even among these people, a considerable degree of social cohesion and mutual aid exists (Hochschild, 1973).

The myth of the factory as a stronghold of depersonalization has also been debunked. The classic work on this topic was carried out by a research team studying the Hawthorne plant of the Western Electric Company in Chicago in the 1930s. This research revealed that work groups tended to develop into cohesive social systems that had a profound influence on workers' morale and even productivity. In particular, members of these informal groups were shown to influence the rate of production on the line by sanctioning fellow workers who deviated too much from an informally set rate (Roethlisberger and Dickson, 1947). Subsequent research has confirmed the power of the informal group to either facilitate or disrupt the workings of formal bureaucracies and to either reinforce or subvert higher authorities (Bensman and Gerver, 1963; Roy, 1972; Stoddard, 1972).

The market, also a prime symbol of depersonalization in contemporary life, is infused with primary groups and their influence. Pioneering work by Lazarsfeld and Katz uncovered what they described as a "two-step flow of influence" in decisions to buy products, attend movies, and the like. Any given community includes certain "influentials," who maintain close touch with national and international advertising. The remainder of the buyers, normally out of touch with or uninfluenced by advertising, are nonetheless influenced personally, largely through informal contact with the influentials in the community (Katz and Lazarsfeld, 1955). A subsequent study of the spread of the use of an antibiotic drug also indicated that one of the most important determinants of whether a physician would adopt the drug was the degree to which he or she interacted with and was influenced by other physicians (Coleman et al., 1966).

Even under circumstances of outright and extreme disorganization, the influence of the primary group persists. Studies of disasters (tornadoes, floods, explosions) show that much of what appears superficially to be panicky or random behavior on the part of community residents is actually interpretable as evidence of their efforts to join or help family and friends elsewhere in the community (Killian, 1952). And in a recent study of a flood disaster in a mining community in West Virginia, whose informal neighborhood and community life had been decimated over the decades by economic hardship and out-migration, Kai Erikson (1976) observed how the absence of primary group ties contributed greatly to the depth and prolongation of the community's subsequent despair and depression.

Studies of drug use have revealed the importance of primary groups in understanding a form of deviant behavior that previously had been thought to be either a consequence of biological vulnerability or the product of forces affecting society at large. Drug use in the contemporary United States is now seen to begin as casual partying behavior among pairs or small groups of close (but generally short-term) high school friends, to continue in a series of casual, mainly adolescent relations, remaining most strongly entrenched when family members, especially siblings or spouses, regularly share drugs, and to decline or end when family or coworker ties not involving drugs are strong. This picture seems to be broadly true of illicit drugs ranging from marijuana (Kandel, 1980) to PCP (Feldman et al., 1979) to heroin (Gould et al., 1974; Hughes, 1977).

THE ANALYSIS OF STATUS ATTAINMENT

The study of social stratification—the unequal distribution of power, privilege, and prestige in society—and social mobility—the stability and change in these attributes from generation to generation and during the life course—was radically transformed with the publication in 1967 of Blau and Duncan's *The American Occupational Structure*. Prior to the work of Duncan and his colleagues, stratification and mobility generally had been conceived as separate phenomena, and the study of social mobility had been concerned mainly with assessing whether American society was becoming less open, that is, whether equality of opportunity was declining. This question was pursued through the analysis of cross-tabulations of father's occupation, divided into roughly hierarchically ordered categories, by son's occupation.

Blau and Duncan reconceptualized mobility as a process of status attainment, in which a father's occupation was but one of many factors—education, occupation, income, and similar attributes—influencing his son's accomplishments. (The initial restriction of analysis to men was strictly a convenience; subsequent research extended the analysis to women and to characteristics of both parents.) Moreover, borrowing statistical procedures developed by the geneticist Sewall Wright (and independently by several econometricians), Blau and Duncan were able to represent and quantify complex processes of status attainment through what are called path models and corresponding systems of structural equations. In this way they moved beyond mere static description of people's status characteristics to a dynamic characterization of the American stratification system (for useful reviews of these developments see Bielby, 1981; Featherman, 1981; and Mare, 1980). For an interesting approach to this work from a life-span perspective, see the paper by Featherman (in Part II).

The creation of scales to measure such concepts as educational attainment and occupational status has been an important part of research in this area. The measurement of occupational status, in particular, has been the subject of an extensive and cumulative research tradition of great theoretical importance. One tradition has focused on the relative prestige of occupations, studying how and why occupations differ in their prestige, demonstrating the essential invariance of occupational prestige hierarchies across time and space (Treiman, 1977), and developing prestige scales to measure the status of occupations (Siegel, 1971; Treiman, 1977). Another tradition has focused on the socioeconomic aspects of occupations as the basis for creating an occupational status scale that is widely used in status attainment research (Duncan, 1961).

The model of status attainment shown in Figure 1 relates father's educational attainment, father's occupational status, son's educational attainment, the status of the son's first job, and the status of the son's job in 1962, the time of the data collection. This model states that a son's educational attainment depends on his father's educational and occupational status (plus a set of unmeasured factors uncorrelated with father's education or occupational status); that the status of the son's first job depends on his own education and his father's occupational status; and that the status of his job in 1962 depends on his education, the status of his first job, and the status of his father's job. The coefficients in the model (which are in fact standardized

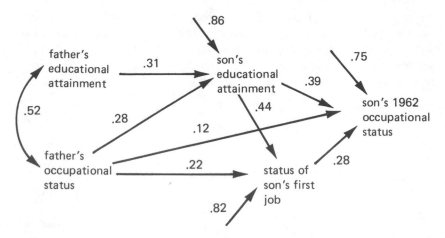

FIGURE 1   Path model of the process of status attainment in the United States, for males from nonfarm origins aged 20 to 64 in 1962. Educational attainment is measured by years of school completed; occupational status is measured by Duncan's Socioeconomic Index (Source: Blau and Duncan, 1967:170). Reprinted by permission of the Free Press, a division of Macmillan Publishing Co., Inc.

regression coefficients estimated from data) indicate the relative importance of these causal connections.

From models such as these it is possible to draw important substantive inferences. Consider the role of education in social mobility. A good deal of both sociological and popular writing in the 1960s portrayed American society as one in which individuals largely inherit their status from their parents and in which the educational system serves mainly as an instrument of status transmission rather than as a means of freeing people from their social origins. Applying the algebra of path analysis to the model shown in Figure 1, Blau and Duncan (1967:200-201) were led to conclude the contrary, that a "very considerable amount of 'status modification' or occupational mobility does occur," and that "far from serving in the main as a factor perpetuating initial status, education operates *primarily* to induce variation in occupational status that is independent of initial status." This is an important conclusion in terms of what it tells us about the structure of American society. And it is by no means intuitively obvious, but is rather a derivation from the model.

This simple five-variable model can hardly be taken as a fully adequate representation of the process of occupational attainment in American society. A great deal of subsequent work has been done to elaborate the model by including additional social origin variables, personality and attitude variables, indicators of the character of the interpersonal environment, and multiple measurements of occupational experience through the course of the career (see in particular Duncan et al., 1972; Jencks et al., 1972; Sewell and Hauser, 1975; Featherman and Hauser, 1978; and Jencks et al., 1979). It is of interest to note that even the elaborated models leave much of the variation in occupational status unexplained. Rather than regarding this as evidence of the inadequacy of the model, however, sociologists regard it as a consequence of the openness of the stratification system of the United States. Would many wish to live in a society in which the occupational attainments of individuals are entirely or even largely determined by their social origins and a handful of additional variables?

Similar models have also been estimated for women and for members of minority groups, and these models have been elaborated in ways that permit systematic comparison of sources of inequality of opportunity and achievement on the basis of race, sex, and ethnic status. Similar procedures have been used to assess trends in opportunity structures and achievement patterns, especially through a careful replication of the 1962 Blau and Duncan study by Featherman and Hauser a decade later (Featherman and Hauser, 1978). Finally, the Blau and Duncan research has served as a model for a number of similar studies conducted in foreign countries. This work will permit systematic comparisons of the process of status attainment in different types of societies, although substantial measurement problems will need to be solved before this becomes a reality.

Work currently under way is beginning to address the relationship between the achievements of individuals and the way educational systems and labor markets are structured to create differential opportunities and incentives for schooling, jobs, and promotions. This work shows promise of providing a much richer description of the processes leading to variations in success in the United States and in other countries.

Much of the power of the modeling procedure used in the study of status attainment—path analysis and structural equation models—derives from its requirement for precise specification of the hypothesized model and its capacity to provide statistical estimates of the adequacy of the model. These requirements make it much easier to understand and to criticize the work of others, even that in other disciplines (e.g., economics), and so have increased the rigor with which theoretical disagreements can be pursued. Perhaps for this reason, these causal modeling procedures have been widely adopted in sociology and other social sciences (see Bielby and Hauser, 1977, for a review of this development).

INFORMATION PROCESSING PSYCHOLOGY

The past quarter century has seen the birth of a new discipline—cognitive science—which encompasses parts of psychology, linguistics, computer science, anthropology, and philosophy and bears a close connection to neuroscience. At the heart of this development was a shift from the behavioristic approach of experimental psychology and its preoccupation with simple memory and learning to an information processing approach and its preoccupation with human thinking and problem solving. For more comprehensive reviews of this topic see National Research Council (1981) and Simon (1980, 1981).

A central aspect of the information processing approach is the use of detailed computer programs to make theories about human problem solving explicit. Two important contributions of this work are (1) the development of computer programs that can make decisions, solve problems, and carry out other processes that in humans we call thinking and (2) the discovery that human thought can be described in terms of programs consisting of the storage, comparison, and manipulation of symbols. Computer simulation of human thinking has done much to release the study of thinking from the hold of vitalism and make it instead a systematic domain of scientific exploration.

One outgrowth of this work is the field known as artificial intelligence, which is concerned with programming computers to "think." Computers have been successfully programmed to play expert or master-level chess, to diagnose disease, to discover reaction paths for the production of organic compounds, and to recognize spoken language. Many of these programs, however, rely on a brute force approach that would be impossible for humans, taking advantage of the size and speed of modern computers to engage in massive searches. In this sense they simulate the function but not the process of thinking, much as airplanes simulate the function but not the process of birds in flight.

Some artificial intelligence programs, however, incorporate what is known about the corresponding human processes, especially strategies that enable humans to be highly selective in their search for solutions. These strategies have been revealed by research analyzing the detailed character of human thinking and problem-solving processes. Much of this research has been conducted by creating computer programs that simulate the process by which humans think, process information, and solve problems. This is done by having human problem solvers "think out loud" about what they do, then programming computers to do similar things and comparing the program in detail with the behavior of the human problem solvers to ensure that the simulation of human behavior is accurate.

An underlying assumption of the information processing approach is that the programs of thought consist of a set of elementary mental operations. Since many of these mental operations are not available to consciousness, the empirical analysis has been an important branch of the field and a major way in which its techniques have received applications in educational, industrial, and medical settings.

To take one example, it is well known that a small amount of information can be stored in a short-term, readily accessible buffer memory. It has been shown that such memory consists of a small number of chunks of information (Simon, 1974). These chunks can be searched at a rate of about 30 milliseconds per chunk (Sternberg, 1966). Individuals differ greatly in the capacity and search rate of this system, but the overall structure appears similar among individuals, over the life-span, and in greatly differing tasks such as mental arithmetic, reading, and chess playing. Much of the increased development of such capacity in early life is due to improved familiarity with the items to be stored (Chi, 1976). It is possible to increase the size of the buffer memory through altering the formation of chunks. One study showed that training could increase the number of digits stored from 7 to about 80 by the development of proper chunking strategies (Chase et al., 1981). Teaching these strategies has been shown to have important effects on the functional memory capacity of both normal and retarded persons (Belmont and Butterfield, 1971). Such chunking strategies greatly improve short-term memory capacity; since they do so uniformly across individuals, however, they are not the source of the differences among people in memory span (Lyon, 1977).

Stored information may be viewed in terms of distinct formats. Thus a written word can activate a visual code, a phonological code, and a complex network of associations, a meaning code (Posner, 1978). In reading it is possible to access the semantic network either from the visual or phonological code. The visual form of the word serves as the major means of unlocking the meaning of the word for most readers, but the phonological code appears necessary for storing information in a way that will lead to understanding the meaning of the passage (Kleiman, 1975). Deaf persons have difficulty in reading largely because they have deficits in representing the phonological structure of the language, and therefore have problems with storage and retrieval. These findings have obvious importance in diagnosing reading difficulty among those who suffer from what is called dyslexia. In striking cases of dyslexia induced by brain injury, the patient may be able to access the meaning and be unable to read the name of a word whose associations he or she knows quite well (Coltheart et al., 1980; see also the paper by Carpenter and Just in Part II on reading as a cognitive process).

While the information processing approach has been productive in linking human cognition to artificial intelligence through the concept of mental programs, it also provides creative opportunities to link cognition to the brain's underlying neural structure. The ability to time-lock elementary mental operations (that is, to identify precisely when one occurs in relation to when others occur) provides a number of experimental techniques for linking cognition and brain processes. It is known that the subjective experience of concentration on a stimulus event increases brain wave activity, as can be indexed in an electroencephalogram in terms of an amplification of components that occur in the first few hundred milliseconds after the stimulus event (Donchin et al., 1978). In the case of spatial attention (that is, recognition of spatial relations), a cognitive capacity that humans share with other organisms, it is possible to examine changes in cellular activity that correspond to the mental operation of shifting attention from one part of the visual field to another. When people shift their eyes to a peripheral visual event, it has been shown that the processing of a target occurring in the neighborhood of that event begins to improve about 200 milliseconds before the eyes start to move (Posner, 1980).

The information processing approach has already led to enhanced understanding of the complex mental performance involved in creativity, memory, language, and the acquisition of other skills (Newell and Simon, 1972; Anderson, 1980). It has also provided a framework that shows promise of guiding explorations in the neural substrate, the functioning of the brain as an information processing system, which has to date proved nearly intractable. As Herbert Simon notes (1981:7):

We have a situation exactly like that in Nineteenth Century chemistry, where a quite elaborate and powerful theory of chemical reactions was built up long before physical theories of atomic structure were available to explain why certain compounds were stable and others unstable; why certain reactions occurred and others did not. As the present situation in the theory of elementary particles also illustrates, this kind of top-down, skyhook support for natural science theories is not at all unusual. If it were not so, the whole structure of scientific knowledge would tremble at each perturbation of the theory of quarks. Thus, cognitive science is concerned with a kind of "mental chemistry," and has made few connections, up to the present moment, with the physiological substratum, which is surely there but whose relations with the symbolic systems it supports are not yet understood. The hope is that understanding of the symbol system will lead to better understanding of the neural substrate, an instance of behavioral research paving the way for physiological research.

ORIGINS OF AGRICULTURE

Studies of the origins of agriculture essentially began in the years following World War II. Earlier archaeological interest in the Near East, in Mesoamerica, and in the central Andes, the regions where these origins are now thought to have occurred, had largely centered on the fully developed civilizations that followed some millennia later. The monumental art, architecture, and (in some cases) historical records left behind by these civilizations were important acquisitions for museums, which sponsored a large part of the archaeological research. By contrast, the transition from food gathering to food production generally left few vestiges suitable for popular exhibit. Yet as a milestone of human achievement it was fully comparable to the rise of urban civilization.

Following the postwar shift of the bulk of archaeological activity from museums to universities, conditions existed for a rapid acceleration of effort on the question of the rise of agriculture. Economic and social development had become a theme of intense comparative study within the social sciences, and this interest extended to archaeological research as well. In a fundamental alteration of viewpoint, archaeologists directed attention away from the study of individual archaeological relics and their stylistic associations and toward the contextual reconstruction of broadly changing patterns of subsistence, technology, and social organization, which lay at the core of the introduction of agriculture. This alteration of viewpoint was facilitated by the favorable opportunities for interdisciplinary work existing in universities and by the support consistently given to such studies by the National Science Foundation.

Most of the major advances in our understanding of the origins of agriculture have depended on the interdisciplinary cooperation of social, biological, and physical scientists. Great improvements in dating techniques (e.g., radiocarbon dating) are probably the most widely known example, but there were developments of comparable importance in other areas as well the analysis of the plant and animal remains of species that became domesticated and analysis of soils, pollen, and other sources of information for environmental reconstruction. Nor were artifacts neglected in these cooperative processes of technical advance. Emphasis has shifted, however, from stylistic analyses of relatively rare complete specimens to analyses of microwear patterns (to understand how tools were used), of the debris of manufacture, and of the behavioral patterns represented by thousands of broken fragments of tools and pottery.

The primary objective of study is no longer the recovery of physical remains, nor even the description of the newly developing technologies associated with extraction, processing, storage, and consumption that were immediately responsible for the successful introduction of agriculture. What is now of greatest interest is the reconstruction of interrelated social and subsistence systems as they evolved over time. Just as the cultural equipment was subject to continuous modification and improvement, so also were the plant and animal species more and more sharply distinguished from their wild prototypes by selective harvesting or breeding. Subsistence strategies and perceptions—of the socially constituted groups adopting them, of the natural world, of risk and opportunity and how to meet them—are and have always been culturally influenced and passed on. For this reason the study of agricultural origins has been primarily organized and conducted by anthropologically oriented archaeologists.

The adoption of food production as an alternative to hunting and gathering is now known to have begun independently in the Old and New Worlds not long after the Pleistocene or Ice Age drew to a close about 12,000 years ago. It appears to have occurred repeatedly and more or less independently in many different settings in both hemispheres, based on locally differentiated complexes of potentially domesticable food resources. There are indications that experimentation along these lines may even have begun some thousands of years earlier in especially favorable settings (e.g., the Nile Valley). Trade-offs were involved in accepting a more sedentary way of life through much of the seasonal cycle in order to promote husbandry, and it seems clear that the productivity and security we associate with agriculture became apparent only very slowly and gradually. Sometimes there is reference to a food-producing revolution, and the term correctly calls attention to the cumulatively decisive change that took place and to its relatively accelerated pace. As an advance that has proved to be in a broad sense irreversible, it certainly bears comparison with the industrial revolution of the late 18th and 19th centuries. But the earlier change is better visualized as a process linking numerous, increasingly complex and interdependent adaptations, rather than as an event proceeding swiftly and self-consciously from a limited series of identifiable discoveries.

The two hearths where the process of conversion to agriculture is currently best understood are the Near East and Mesoamerica. Others, not yet so well documented but quite possibly of comparable antiquity, are in Southeast Asia and probably in China, East Africa, and tropical South America. The Near East was, on the basis of current evidence, the earliest locus. Coinciding with a period of climatic and vegetational shifts, settled village farming communities had made their appearance there by about 9,000 years ago. The region of earliest cultivation of the wild grasses that were the progenitors of modern wheat and barley lay immediately east of the Mediterranean, while at about the same time sheep and goats may have been first domesticated along the flanks of the Zagros and Taurus mountains somewhat farther east. Additional crops and domestic animals were added to these over several succeeding millennia.

The Mesoamerican equivalent of this process is best known from south central Mexico, where morphological changes in the remains of 9,000-year-old squash suggest the beginnings of domestication. Domestic maize and beans appeared two millennia or so later, but maize, in particular, required several millennia of further selective breeding before great enlargement of the ears and kernels permitted it to serve as the foundation of subsistence for American Indians. Numerous fruits and vegetables were gradually added to the food crop complex. Domesticated animals were of minor importance in most New World areas until the coming of the Spaniards in the 16th century.

Most social scientists today have grown increasingly dubious about the adequacy of simple, single-cause explanations for anything, and the archaeologists among them are no exception. Few of those specializing in this subject believe that there is any single factor, or even closely related set of factors, that was repeatedly responsible for the initial introduction and subsequent spread of an agricultural way of life. One of the earliest plausible suggestions was that the enforced propinquity of humans and potential domesticates along the fringes of shrinking oases initiated a successful process of experimentation leading to husbandry. This hypothesis assumed that climatic change was a factor, an assumption that finds at least partial support in a number of converging lines of scientific evidence, although shrinking oases are no longer seen as a likely locus. The propinquity of human groups and potential domesticates is an obvious precondition (thus helping to locate some of the hearths) but not an explanation. More recent work has tended to focus on zones in which wild subsistence resources were subject to periodic, critical interruption, intensifying pressures for innovations that would provide greater security regarding food supplies. According to another hypothesis, relatively more permanent, year-round settlements were first dictated by other components of the food quest, such as a dependence on fishing or shellfishing. This led in turn to attempts to develop a new subsistence base with a greatly amplified range and quantity of localized food resources.

Population pressure plays a part in a number of the causal explanations that are being tentatively advanced. It is an exceedingly difficult concept to test within the constraints of the fragmentary archaeological record, but it does direct attention to the special incentives for technological and other innovation that must have existed under changing, uncertain, or otherwise marginal conditions. Also evident in a number of current theoretical approaches are applications of positive and negative feedback principles derived from modern systems theory. As this overview suggests, the field is in a state of active advance (for reviews of these developments see Flannery, 1973; Bender, 1975; Megaw, 1977; and Reed, 1977). There is widespread debate over divergent explanations and unassimilated data, and it is premature to speak of an emerging consensus around a single synthesis. But it can also be said that a major, previously unrevealed chapter of human existence has been at least roughly blocked out, within the space of a single generation of scientific effort.

SOCIAL CHOICE

Social choice theory focuses on the identification and analysis of various principles by which groups or entire societies do, might, or should decide what policies to adopt. Can we speak meaningfully about the welfare of society as a whole, as distinct from that of the individuals who compose a society? This question has occupied philosophers since antiquity and is the principal subject matter of two areas of contemporary social science—welfare economics and axiomatic social choice theory. In economics the issue is to analyze economic arrangements in terms of their relative benefit to the totality of people in society; in political science the main interest is to analyze different voting systems, ranging from committee decision-making processes to national elections, to understand how individual preferences are translated into a collective or social choice. Reviews of this area are available in Mueller (1976), Plott (1976), and Russell (1979).

A central problem of social choice theory is how to reconcile the desires, values, and interests of different individuals and groups when they are not in agreement, which is taken by social choice theorists as synonymous with the question of how to decide what is of greatest benefit to society as a whole. The problem is most easily seen with respect to the analysis of voting systems. In the United States we are used to thinking of majority rule as an attractive voting system, partly because it appears to treat both candidates and voters in a neutral and unbiased fashion. In a majority rule system the social decision should coincide with whatever preference is held by a majority of voters. Yet it can be shown that if there are more than two alternatives available, it may not be possible to determine the majority choice unambiguously.

Consider the following situation, with three voters (1, 2, 3) and three choices (candidates Reagan, Anderson, Carter). Suppose voter 1 thinks Reagan is best, Anderson is second best, and Carter is third best; whereas the preference order of voter 2 is Anderson, Carter, Reagan; and the preference order of voter 3 is Carter, Reagan, Anderson. Under these circumstances we have a paradoxical social choice: Reagan is preferred to Anderson (since a majority, voters 1 and 3, prefer Reagan to Anderson); at the same time Anderson is preferred to Carter, and, also, Carter is preferred to Reagan. In other words, no alternative is best in the sense that it is unambiguously preferred to all other alternatives. This violates a common assumption, transitivity, which requires that if a is preferred to b and b is preferred to c, then a will be preferred to c. It turns out that this problem is endemic to virtually all voting systems that treat voters and alternatives neutrally. One way out of the dilemma would seem to be to vote on each

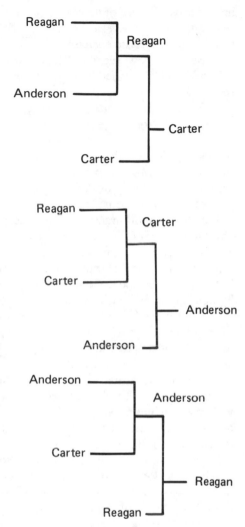

FIGURE 2 Three different orders of voting lead to three inconsistent choices for winner.

pair of options successively. But this would not resolve the dilemma, since the outcome will be seen to depend entirely on the order of voting:

1. If voters first choose between Reagan and Anderson, Reagan's two favorable votes will win out over Anderson's one favorable vote. Then, when the winner Reagan is pitted against Carter, Carter's two favorable votes against Reagan's one will render Carter the final winner. (If this example is

unpersuasive because of the actual election outcome, think back to 1964 and substitute Goldwater, Rockefeller, and Johnson. But mostly keep in mind that this is an analytic exercise.)

2. Suppose, however, that Reagan was first pitted against Carter. Again, he would win. But when he is in turn pitted against Anderson, Anderson is seen to win.

3. Finally, had we first pitted Anderson against Carter, Reagan would be the ultimate victor.

In short, as Figure 2 demonstrates, we see that the alternative that is omitted from the first of the two votes always wins. So the paradox is not resolved, since there is no way of deciding which of the three possible orderings of pairs of votes is to be preferred.

The dilemma illustrated by the three-person, three-choice situation has obvious implications for the American presidential electoral system. Although our electoral system is somewhat more complex, with choices among candidates in primary elections followed by a choice between primary winners in the general election, the dilemma is much more general—as was shown by Kenneth Arrow in his *impossibility theorem* (1963). What Arrow showed is that under a set of plausible assumptions that most of us would readily agree to and that most designers of voting systems have taken for granted (e.g., the assumption of preference transitivity, mentioned above; the assumption that preferences between any two choices do not depend on what other options are available; and the assumption that individuals are free to select any choice of ordering), and if society must make choices in a wide variety of circumstances, then the society's choice must be that of a single one of the voters or it must be imposed from the outside; in other words, the only way to get a definitive social choice is through dictatorship.

Were Arrow's theorem simply a mathematical curiosity, it could easily be dismissed as of interest only to scholars. The difficulty is that the assumptions that lead necessarily to Arrow's impossibility theorem are shared, implicitly or explicitly, by virtually all believers in democracy and are encountered in most actual voting systems. In consequence, Arrow's work, for which he won the 1972 Nobel prize in economics, has stimulated a great deal of subsequent analysis and research. This work is divided into three main categories: attempts to discredit the main theorem by challenging some of its assumptions; mathematical analysis of choice systems that operate under different assumptions; and empirical research on the behavior of actual voting and choice systems, although much of this latter research has had quite independent origins. (For a review of some of the latter material, see the paper by Converse et al. in Part II.) One major contribution of social choice theory thus far has been to challenge older understandings derived from political theory about the operation of voting and other choice systems and to clarify the assumptions underlying such systems. The field is moving very rapidly and it is difficult to predict future developments. As is common with landmark breakthroughs in understanding, social choice theory is being shown by current researchers to apply to important areas of life that would seem remote from voting. For example, how can society devise cheat-proof methods of auctioning to determine the scope of public-goods programs (lighthouses, fire stations, defense and security systems)? These important questions turn out to be logically identical to the social choice calculus of Arrow, Vickery, and other social scientists.

HUMAN ORIGINS

Theories of human origins have been vigorously debated for more than 100 years. Although most scientists agree that humans evolved from some earlier form of primate, until very recently there was little consensus on when the hominid lineage became separate from other animals. The differences of opinion were substantial. Some believed that our ancestors were apes, similar to the chimpanzee or gorilla; others maintained that there never was an apelike creature in our ancestry. Some thought the human-nonhuman sepa ration was recent (4 or 5 million years ago), while others thought it was ancient (more than 40 million years ago). The radically different opinions of competent scientists made it evident that neither comparative anatomy nor the fossil record could settle the issues.

Since the 1960s a variety of biochemical methods have been developed that made it possible to compare humans to other contemporary mammals by quantitative methods — immunology, electrophoresis, sequences of amino acids in proteins, and direct comparisons of the genetic substance, DNA (Goodman and Tashian, 1976). For a general review of this topic, see the September 1978 issue of *Scientific American*, subsequently published by W. H. Freeman (Isaac and Leakey, 1979).

The main outlines of primate evolution revealed by these methods are shown in Figure 3. In order to simplify and summarize a large amount of information, the genetically measured distance between humans and chimpanzees is taken as 1. The numbers on the chart refer to this distance. The time of the separation of the various lines is calculated from molecular divergences. For example, the human-chimpanzee separation is estimated as 5-8 million years ago, the human-orangutan separation as 10-16 million years ago, and the monkey-human separation as 20-25 million years ago. Although there is not yet complete consensus on these dates, they are considered reasonable approximations and show clearly the close relationship of hominids and African apes (chimpanzees and gorillas).

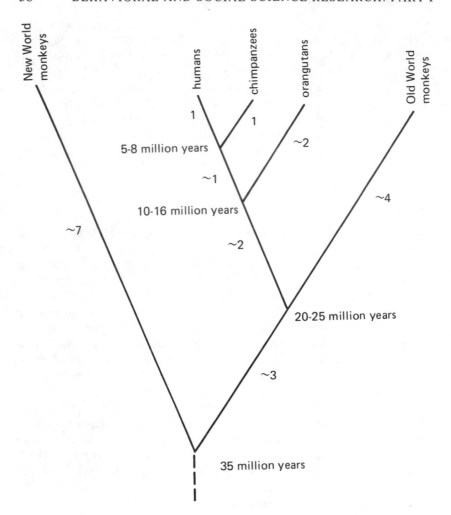

FIGURE 3   Diagram of human evolution. The numbers refer to the evolutionary distance between chimpanzees and human beings.

The rates of evolution for some proteins are remarkably constant, and some portions of DNA also appear to evolve at constant rates. Genetically, small prosimians, tree shrews, monkeys, apes, and human beings have all changed approximately the same amount since the primates became a separate order of mammals. The amount of certain kinds of genetic change correlates with time—not with number of young, length of generation, or morphological change. These findings suggest that a significant portion of the genome (the body of genetic information that determines heredity) is not subject to natural selection but rather changes in a random way at a steady rate. Much change at the molecular level may be explained by this neutral theory of evolution; the relative importance of selection and neutral factors in evolution is a field of major controversy at the present time (Kimura, 1979).

All the biochemical findings of the last few years support the beliefs that humans and the African apes are very closely related, that humans and the apes had a long period of common ancestry, and that apes and monkeys shared a long common ancestry before that. The main outline is not new; what is new is being able to base the theory on molecular information and eliminate theories that demand a very early separation of the human line. This is a major clarification—almost no scientists believed that apes and humans are as close as they have proved to be.

The fossil record of the early stages of hominid and nonhominid primate evolution is growing steadily. New techniques of anatomical analysis and new knowledge about living biological systems (from complex social systems to simple anatomical ones) are fleshing out the ancient bones, enabling us to see the extinct as the once alive.

The earliest definite fossil evidence for hominids comes from the footsteps found by Mary Leakey and coworkers at Laetoli, Tanzania. The footsteps, more than 3.5 million years old, document a typically human bipedality. Fossils of a comparable age have been found by Donald Johanson and coworkers in Ethiopia. These hominids had small brains, no larger than those of contemporary apes, walked upright, and probably did not make stone tools. These finds support the evidence of the fossil finds in South Africa many years ago, which showed that human locomotion evolved long before human brains enlarged significantly. Judging by the behavior of chimpanzees and the hands and teeth of the fossils, the small-brained bipeds (*Australopithecus*) were probably using tools, although perhaps not making patterned tools from durable materials. Stone tools appear in the fossil record by 2.5 million years ago, but the time is uncertain. In the period 2 million to 1 million years ago, stone tools were present, at first in simplest form, but becoming quite advanced. During this million-year period the brain doubled in size and *Homo erectus* replaced the earlier forms. *Homo erectus*, who occupied much of the Old World, made complex stone tools, killed large animals, and controlled fire. But technical progress was exceedingly slow—the same kinds of tools were made for hundreds of thousands of years (Washburn, 1979).

By about 40,000 years ago, people anatomically like us had appeared, possibly by rapid spread from a quite restricted area. Then progress accelerated;

these modern humans spread all over the world. They crossed large bodies of water, reached Australia, adapted to life in the Arctic, and finally entered the New World. Art, housing, compound tools, boats, fishing, and tailored clothing all appear in the record of technological acceleration. It is tempting to think that this great acceleration was the result of communication, of language as we know it. There must have been earlier and simpler forms, but these have left no trace in the archaeological record. This latest phase of human evolution, in which we know that human nature was basically the same as it is today, represents less than 1 percent of uniquely human evolution (measuring from the time after our ancestors separated from the apes).

Five million years is a small part of the total history of life on earth. In these 5 million years humans became bipedal, became skillful with their hands, became hunters and warriors, and began to control nature. Evolution produced a brain capable of learning those behaviors important for surviva in the distant past. It is this biological ability to learn that is the most important aspect of human nature. The ability is old, a product of evolution, but what we learn is new, a product of the last few hundred years, particularly of sciences; and how we learn it is also new.

When considering human evolution, it is very important to remember that the evidence is changing. Science is not static, and the study of human evolution is no exception. Progress is under way and can be expected to accelerate in many areas. The fossil evidence accumulates at an increasing rate, and our ability to make sense of it, to produce descriptions and explanations of past adaptations, expands as our application of what we learn from studies of living animals becomes more sophisticated. Twenty years ago the dates given for fossils were informed guesses. Today there is a series of methods (potassium-argon, magnetic reversals, fission track) that yields accurately determined dates not dependent on any single individual's opinion. Molecular biology has revolutionized methods of comparing animals and has greatly changed evolutionary theory. Jerold Lowenstein (1980) has shown that there may be enough unaltered protein left in fossil bones so that these methods can be directly applied to some fossils, which holds promise of definitively settling ongoing arguments about relationships between various fossils and leading to much firmer conclusions from the fossil record.

SOCIAL BEHAVIOR OF MONKEYS AND APES

Despite centuries of fascination with monkeys and apes, reflecting intuitive recognition of their close relationship to humans, until very recently almost nothing was known about the behavior of nonhuman primates in their natural habitats. In the late 1950s a series of field studies was initiated by zoologists, psychologists, and anthropologists motivated by concerns ranging from an attempt to understand the origins of human behavior to an interest in the functioning of small groups. In the past 30 years the study of the behavior of nonhuman primates has rapidly developed into one of the most sophisticated and productive areas of research at the interface between the biological and social sciences.

The study of nonhuman primate behavior falls into four interrelated areas: social behavior and development, social organization, ecology and life history patterns, and intelligence. Some examples illustrate the sorts of problems that primatologists address.

In his famous experiments on monkeys raised in isolation, the psychologist Harry F. Harlow showed that young monkeys who are denied contact with other monkeys develop into listless, hollow parodies of their group-raised, socially adept peers (Harlow and Harlow, 1962, 1965). Long-term field studies of individually recognized animals make clear why this is so: Primate infants, helpless at birth, depend for months or even years on their mothers for survival (Altmann, 1980). This dependence is reflected in a prolonged emotional bond between mother and infant. In the wild the intensity of this bond is most clearly revealed after death: Monkey mothers whose infants die often carry the body for days, repeatedly staring at the lifeless form with a dazed expression. Chimpanzees orphaned before the age of five sink rapidly into a severe depressive response characterized by loss of appetite, absence of response to environmental stimuli, and stereotypic body movements. Most orphans recover, but some die soon after their mothers, due in part at least to their depressed condition.

Many aspects of nonhuman primate social organization were not understood until groups of recognized individuals had been observed for a number of years (Hamburg and McCown, 1979). Perhaps the most important finding to emerge from long-term field studies is the fact that all monkeys and apes live with close kin and that group social organization is based on kinship ties. In most species, females remain in the group of their birth, whereas males leave at adolescence. In these species, lifelong relationships among females linked through a common female ancestor are the key to group structure (Kurland, 1977; Wrangham, 1980). In a few species, including our closest relative, the chimpanzee, males remain in their natal groups and females leave; in this case the kinship group is based on father-son and brother-brother ties. In all nonhuman primates that have been well studied, it is clear that individuals form their strongest and most persistent bonds with close relatives and that they cooperate with these relatives against unrelated individuals from other groups. Blood ties form the fabric of nonhuman primate society.

Detailed studies of the activity patterns of nonhuman primates in natural habitats have shown that they approximate an optimal balance between energy expended (in survival and reproduction) and energy obtained through food. All aspects of the life of a nonhuman primate—its movements, its interactions with others, the kind of group it lives in, the timing of sexual maturity, reproduction and old age (life history patterns)—are reflections of the nature and distribution of its food resources (Richard, 1981). Several long-term studies that covered periods of naturally occurring food scarcity show that monkeys reacted immediately to changed conditions: Average weights decreased, age at first reproduction went up, morbidity and mortality increased dramatically—the very old, the very young, and those low in dominance and therefore least able to compete for food were hit the hardest (Glander, 1977).

Parallel studies in the laboratory on the effects of different nutritional regimens on maternal milk production, infant growth and development, infant mortality, and maternal mortality have expanded our understanding of the fine line that exists between a well-fed and an undernourished mother-infant pair. Because the diets, digestive physiology, social organization, and life history patterns of many nonhuman primates are similar to our own, they provide ideal subjects for studying the effects of a changed environment on behaviors associated with survival and reproduction.

The earliest research on nonhuman primates in captivity focused on ape intelligence, and recently primatologists have returned to this subject. American sign language, the gestural language of the deaf, has been taught to over a dozen chimpanzees, gorillas, and orangutans, and several have learned over 500 of its "words." Although scientists disagree as to whether the apes' usage of sign language constitutes true language, these animals clearly have a capacity for symbolic communication that has amazed (and delighted) everyone who comes into contact with them.

These studies are of interest for two reasons. First, they allow us to conduct experiments on the process of language acquisition that for ethical reasons cannot be done using human children. Second, American sign language provides a medium of communication between human and ape that allows us to see into the minds of another species—an accomplishment that, 15 years ago, would have seemed credible only in a science fiction novel. Human paleontologists now believe that the human ancestor who first walked upright, made tools, and invented spoken language had a brain very much like that of the living apes (see the discussion of human origins above and also Lovejoy, 1981). Thus a better understanding of their minds is one of the most promising avenues of research for shedding light on the origins of the most awesome human attribute, the brain.

4

The Uses of Social and Behavioral Research

Just as our everyday lives have been transformed by computer chips, communications satellites, and advances in medical technology, so, too, have they been transformed by public opinion polls, standardized tests, demographic projections, and human factors engineering. Moreover, our notions about ourselves and each other—about racial differences, for example, or the nature of childhood—have been radically transformed by the dissemination of social and behavioral research findings.

This chapter reviews a few of these developments. We stress once again, however, that a comprehensive account covering the entire range of such developments is beyond the scope of this or any single report. The chapter is divided into three sections. The first reviews three inventions that are used to generate information necessary for planning, analysis, and decision making: sample surveys, standardized tests, and economic models. The second section reviews a variety of changes in practice resulting from behavioral and social research findings. The third section reviews the way social and behavioral research contributes to conceptual change, altering the ideas and understandings we have about ourselves and our society.

INFORMATION-GENERATING TECHNOLOGIES

A major contribution of the social and behavioral sciences has been the invention and development of information-generating technologies. Much has been written about the information revolution, made possible by the development of high-speed computers. Equally important, perhaps, is the ethos of our society that places high value on informed decision making and informed public discussion of alternative possibilities. Given that we are a large and diverse society with complex economic, political, and social institutions, extensive information is needed to inform decisions and to analyze their effects. It is difficult to imagine how either government or business could function these days without economic indicator data. Dependence on a variety of social and political data is nearly as great. Accordingly, there has been and continues to be great impetus for the development of improved information bases and improved decision-making procedures, and basic research in the social sciences has played a central role in these developments. Here we review three technologies developed by social and behavioral scientists: the sample survey, the standardized test, and econometric forecasting models.

SAMPLE SURVEYS

Perhaps the single most important information-generating invention of the social sciences is the sample survey, developed over the course of the past 50 years by statisticians, sociologists, economists, political scientists, psychometricians, and survey specialists. Sample surveys consist of the collection of data in a standardized format, usually from a probability sample of a population.[1] Major advances in the technology of data collection and in probability sampling procedures have made it possible to collect systematic data on the behavior and attitudes of the American people as a whole, and on specific subgroups, with great efficiency and at relatively low cost.[2] These advances include the development of household sampling frames and cluster sampling techniques; the elaboration of the standard personal interview to questionnaires, telephone interviewing, and structured personal diaries; the

---

[1]A probability sample is one for which there is a specified probability that each case in the population will be included in the sample. The most basic kind of probability sample is a simple random sample, in which each member of the population has an equal probability of being chosen for the sample. Usually, more complex designs are used. For example, because there are fewer blacks than other racial groups in the population, blacks are sometimes sampled at a higher rate than others to ensure that the sample includes the minimum number of blacks necessary to achieve reliable estimates. In addition, sometimes samples are designed with multiple stages to reduce data collection costs: First cities are sampled, with their probability of being included in the sample proportional to their population size; then sections of the city are sampled; then blocks within sections; then households within blocks; and finally persons within households.

[2]Suppose, for example, that we wanted to estimate the proportion of the population of the United States that is Roman Catholic from an item on religious identification in a national sample survey of 1,500 people. If we were to take many simple random samples, each of 1,500 people, and if the true proportion of Roman Catholics were 25 percent, then 95 percent of all

sampling of administrative records, past and present; and data collection in experimental settings, especially large-scale social experiments (see the paper in Part II by Tanur for a review of some of these developments; see also Deming, 1968, and Stuart, 1968, on sampling). As a result, the sample survey has become for some social scientists what the telescope is to astronomers, the accelerator to physicists, and the microscope to biologists— the principal instrument of data collection for basic research purposes. This is not to say that sample survey procedures are without difficulties. There is currently lively debate in the research literature about the reliabilty and validity of survey responses and about the efficacy of alternative procedures; see, for example, the National Research Council report *Survey Measurement of Subjective Phenomena* (Turner and Martin, 1981).

The value of the sample survey extends beyond its use by social scientists. It has become the major source of information for a wide variety of public and private purposes, and as a consequence has become a highly marketable technology. Most information collected by federal, state, and local governments for planning and policy-making purposes depends on sample survey methodology. The statistical systems of most industrialized nations, which provide information on health, housing, education, welfare, commerce, industry, etc., are constructed largely on the methodology of sample surveys (see Keyfitz, 1968, Hauser, 1975).

One form of data of particular value for information purposes is statistical time series, in which measurements of a given phenomenon are made repeatedly at successive points in time—monthly, quarterly, annually, decennially, etc. We now have fairly long series for a number of social and economic phenomena, some running 100 years or more but most dating from the 1950s or later. The accumulation of time series data enables us to discern important social and economic trends and hence to monitor social change. In addition to a variety of well-known economic indicators (e.g., the gross national product and the consumer price index, among many others), good time series data are available on the test performance of high school and college students, health and disease rates, labor force participation rates, trends in labor force structure, and subjective phenomena, such as levels of

---

of the samples would have an estimated proportion of Roman Catholics between 22.8 and 27.2 percent. Clearly the size of the error in any given sample is unknown—if the true proportion were known, we wouldn't need a sample survey. However, the variability over all possible samples can be estimated from the variation in a single sample survey of a given size. Larger samples yield more accurate results. For example, for samples of 6,000 people, 95 percent of all of the samples would have an estimated proportion of Roman Catholics between 23.9 and 26.1 percent. Thus, increasing the sample by a factor of 4 decreases the interval of results by a factor of 2.

alienation, trust in government, and racial attitudes, to name only a few. Such data not only provide information for policy deliberations but also alert us as to what needs attention if we are to understand social change.

Sample surveys are also widely used in the private sector, where market research has become an indispensable tool to discover consumer preferences for everything from cars to candidates. No major election is now conducted without extensive polling of the electorate, a specialized form of market research. Public opinion polling has also emerged as a crucial part of the apparatus of modern journalism—a way for newspapers and news magazines to take and report the pulse of the nation. If the pervasiveness of public opinion polling is, like television, a mixed blessing, it is also, like television, an integral part of modern life.

One particularly important analytic use of sample survey data is making population projections. Based on techniques developed by demographers (see the paper by Menken and Trussell in Part II), projections are now routinely made of the future size and characteristics of the population of neighborhoods, cities, regions, and the nation as a whole. Commercial enterprises make heavy use of such data in decisions about where to locate offices, factories, and retail outlets and about the kinds of products to produce and the nature of the marketing strategy to follow. Local governments make similar use of such data in decisions about where to locate schools, hospitals, and other facilities and in planning for the future. The ability to anticipate increases or decreases in the tax base, school enrollments, the demand for bilingual education, homes for the elderly, the balance of social security contributions and payments, and so on all depend on population projections based in part on sample survey data.

Applied survey research directly depends on methods and techniques developed in the course of basic research in the social sciences. Indeed, it would be fair to say that survey research techniques have advanced parallel to the advances of empirical social science over the past four decades. To be sure, there was extensive interaction between basic and applied concerns from the earliest days of serious survey research in the 1930s, when both Roper and Gallup began their polls and when Paul Lazarsfeld, the father of survey research as we know it, initiated his research program at Columbia University. Almost all of the methodological and conceptual advances came from university research centers—the Bureau of Applied Social Research directed by Lazarsfeld at Columbia, the National Opinion Research Center at the University of Chicago, and the Survey Research Center at the University of Michigan. The history of voting research (reviewed in the paper by Converse et al. in Part II), in particular, is almost inseparable from the history of survey research. Similarly, microeconomics is almost entirely dependent on survey data (see the paper by Heckman and Michael in Part

II), as is the study of social stratification and mobility in sociology and the study of attitude formation and attitude change in social psychology, to name just a few.

One of the things social scientists use sample surveys for is to establish empirical regularities in attitudes, behavior, and social processes. Such empirical regularities—for example, the stable pattern of age-related mortality in all societies, the differential voter turnout between presidential and off-year elections, the relative invariance in markedly different societies of hierarchies of occupational prestige, the division of labor by gender, and the lower earnings of women in all industrial societies—provide the building stones for theories of social structure and social process and constitute information that can inform choices made by individuals and organizations. For example, age-related mortality rates have important implications for public health programs in developing societies, and differential voter turnout has implications for campaign strategies and electoral reform.

STANDARDIZED TESTING

Next to the sample survey, probably no other invention of the social sciences has had as far reaching an impact on American life as the standardized ability test. While systematic testing procedures have had a very long history (the civil service examinations in imperial China are a classic example), standardized quantitative tests based on psychometric scaling principles are a relatively recent development.

Toward the end of the 19th century, psychologists began to show serious interest in individual differences and their measurement. While much of the early work concentrated on the measurement of simple sensory and motor functions, there was considerable interest in the measurement of mental functions such as memory, judgment, and intelligence. Most early efforts to devise mental tests proved unsatisfactory, however, for want of a metric for calibrating "intelligence" and other mental functions. A major breakthrough was achieved in 1908 by the French psychologist Alfred Binet, who developed a test to assist the French Ministry of Public Instruction in identifying retarded schoolchildren (Binet and Simon, 1908). The key to Binet's test is that it measured individual development against a standard of "normal" development for children of the same age, thus solving the calibration problem. The measure of intelligence used, the intelligence quotient (or IQ), was defined as

$$IQ = \frac{\text{mental age}}{\text{chronological age}} \times 100.$$

Thus, for example, a child of 10 who could answer questions and solve problems as well as the average child of 13 would be said to have a mental age of 13 and hence an IQ of 130. The Binet test was adapted for use in the United States by Lewis Terman of Stanford University and became known as the Stanford-Binet, the most famous of all tests of intelligence (Terman, 1916).

Perhaps because the early 20th century was a period of great social change in the United States, in which the need for "objective" assessment procedures was widely felt, ability and achievement tests of all kinds were rapidly and widely adopted. Aptitude tests were devised to assist in the classification of students in order to channel them into various educational tracks. Achievement tests were devised for the certification of student performance and the evaluation of instructional programs. Tests of both general abilities and specific skills were developed for use in employment screening, and similar tests were created for the classification and allocation of army recruits. Standardized testing was given additional impetus during World War II by the need to classify draftees efficiently, and still later by the need of colleges and universities to select from among an excess of applicants created by the postwar baby boom. Today the use of such tests has become so widespread that there are probably few Americans who have not had substantial experience with them.

From its earliest beginnings the testing industry has relied heavily on psychometric theory and methods, and as psychometric research has progressed standardized tests have become more sophisticated. Of course, as in so many other areas, the process was interactive—much of the impetus for the development of psychometric techniques stemmed from the need to improve testing procedures. Developments have occurred in two major areas: the statistical theory of measurement and practical procedures for test construction.

As an example of the first area, procedures have been devised for assessing and improving the reliability and validity of tests. *Reliability* indicates the extent to which a phenomenon can be measured without error; usually this is assessed by ascertaining the similarity of results yielded by alternate forms of a test. *Validity* indicates the extent to which the test measures what one thinks it measures. There are different types of validity and reliability, but one example will suffice. The purpose of college admissions tests ordinarily is to distinguish between those who are likely to be successful in college and those who are not. The test can be said to be valid insofar as those who score well do better in college than those who score poorly. It can be said to be reliable if different subsets of questions yield similar rankings of candidates, the implication being that scores are not strongly affected by the idiosyncrasies of particular questions.

Practical test construction procedures also have been improved substantially. For example, group testing has largely replaced individual testing, thus improving efficiency. Much attention has been devoted to the development of procedures for calibrating or "norming" tests (age has been largely abandoned as a standard, since many abilities have been shown not to vary systematically with age). And there is greater understanding of how the test-taking situation can affect performance.

Contemporary standardized tests have three main uses: selection, classification, and diagnosis. Although these uses shade into each other, they are analytically distinct. A major use of standardized tests is to select from a group of candidates those best suited to an activity and most likely to succeed at it. Admissions tests and personnel selection tests are examples. A second use is for classification. Selection shades into classification when the purpose is to match people to one of several activities or programs. The use of IQ tests to place students in "fast," "regular," and "slow" classes is an example, as is the use of aptitude tests by the army to assign recruits to various training programs. The use of achievement tests to identify a student's areas of strength and weakness and to monitor remedial programs is an example of the third use, diagnosis, as is the use of vocational interest inventories to counsel individuals regarding the suitability of alternative career choices.

It is probably fair to say that the impact of standardized testing has been generally positive, contributing to more informed decisions about educational and vocational choices, to more efficient allocation of people to activities for which they are well suited, and hence to the enhanced realization of human potential. Arguments supporting this view are to be found in Cronbach (1970), Buros (1972), and Anastasi (1976), which provide comprehensive summaries of the literature assessing the contribution of standardized testing.

Standardized testing is not without its critics, however, and its history is not without blemishes. Although the intent of Binet's work in France had been to identify the mentally retarded *in order to provide remedial instruction and by so doing to improve mental performance*, Binet's conception of human intellect as malleable did not survive transatlantic passage. The testing movement succumbed to the hereditarian and racist assumptions endemic to early 20th-century American culture. Ethnic group differences in mental abilities, documented by the wholesale testing of army recruits during World War I (Yerkes, 1921), were taken as evidence of innate national differences in ability (rather than as a straightforward reflection of differences in average length of residence in the United States and average levels of schooling) and were used as the intellectual basis for the National Origins Act of 1924, which established immigration quotas.

Beginning in the 1930s an environmentalist ethos began to replace the hereditarian one, and group differences in test performance came to be generally recognized as reflecting features of the intellectual environment. At the individual level, however, testing was seen as a tool for promoting meritocracy, a device for identifying talented members of the society and for efficiently allocating society's intellectual resources to various educational opportunities and occupational slots. Still later the question was raised as to whether group differences in average test scores reflect not only environmental differences but also bias in the tests themselves, a tendency for tests to underestimate the capabilities of members of disadvantaged minorities. The tension between the positive functions of tests and their potential bias with respect to particular groups continues today; it is reviewed in a recent National Research Council report, *Ability Testing: Uses, Consequences, and Controversies* (Wigdor and Garner, 1982). An important finding of that report is that ability tests are not biased against minorities; that is, on the whole they predict the performance of minorities as well and as accurately as they do for members of the majority population. The report recognizes, however, that the absence of test bias does not exhaust the questions of fairness raised by test use.

ECONOMIC DATA AND ECONOMIC MODELS

Despite obvious political differences about how to cure economic ills, most economic decision makers both inside and outside the government share a reliance on a set of economic indicators and decision tools that are the product of economic research conducted since World War I. It is hard to imagine how the economies of the United States and other industrialized nations could function today without the kind of economic information that is now routinely available.

Economic Data

Contemporary economic data are characterized by their integration into a coherent framework representing the functioning of the economy as a whole. The basic idea that the functioning of the economy depends on the interaction of its parts was introduced by John Maynard Keynes in *The General Theory of Employment, Interest and Money* (1936). Prior to the work of Keynes, economic series were created largely independently of one another and hence were difficult to interpret in relation to one another. Stimulated by Keynes's theoretical work, economists in the United States and Europe developed a comprehensive set of economic indicators covering all aspects of production, consumption, saving, and investment for the economy as a whole. Important work was done by Kuznets (1941) and others on national income accounts, showing transactions among these sectors. This is the work that gave rise to the concept of gross national product (GNP) and many other familiar economic indicators. In a related development, Leontief (1941) invented a way of analyzing the inputs and outputs of specific industrial sectors of the economy in relation to one another. Meanwhile, work had been progressing on the theory of index numbers, with a major contribution by Fisher in 1922. An index number measures the magnitude of a variable relative to some specified level of the variable. Thus, if we take the price of a candy bar in a given year as our standard, and it costs 25 cents that year and 30 cents a year later, the index for the cost of the candy bar in the second year would be 120 (= 100 x 30/25). Index numbers for single commodities present no problems, but considerable complication is introduced when one aggregates several commodities whose prices are changing in different ways, as for example in the construction of the consumer price index. Fisher worked out a consistent set of principles for carrying out such aggregations.

The result of these efforts has been the generation of a large number of economic time series that are mutually consistent and analytically coherent. An adequate data base was a necessary precondition to the development of models of the functioning of the economy as a whole; such models have been widely used both for forecasting short-run changes in the economy and for assessing the impact of various proposed economic policies.

Econometric Forecasting

Economies like that of the United States are highly complex and relatively volatile, fluctuating as a result of the interaction of specific events and policy manipulations. Given this, it used to be extremely difficult to predict short-run changes in the economy with accuracy. While it still is not possible to predict such changes with complete accuracy, the development of computer data bases and of large-scale models of the U.S. economy (and now of other economies as well) has substantially improved prediction, so much so that economic forecasting has become a substantial industry both in the United States and abroad, with a commercial market exceeding $100 million in the United States (Klein, 1980).

Econometric macroeconomic models consist of dozens to hundreds of equations that must be solved simultaneously (one model consists of more than 2,000 equations), each equation representing the interrelationship of particular facets of the economy. For example, one equation in the model might specify how the level of future consumption depends on changes in the level of disposable income of consumers, while another equation might specify how changes in disposable income depend, on the average, on levels of national output, taxation, etc. These models are used to predict the future course of the economy by projecting trends in various economic indicators and by using the model to estimate the effects on them of alternative policy measures and of still other variables. The models are also used to predict the response of the economy to such perturbations and shocks as increased oil prices, military action, taxation, manipulation of the money supply, worldwide speculation in raw materials, etc. The sorts of responses that are predicted are changes in inflation, interest, and unemployment rates, among others.

The utility of these models was established early when they began to yield predictions that ran counter to, but proved more correct than, the conventional economic wisdom of the time. A crude model constructed by Klein in 1946, for example (Maugh, 1980:758),

contradicted widespread predictions that the postwar economy would fall into another depression. The standard view at the time was that there would be as many as 6 million unemployed people in this country. Klein's model, however, indicated that there was a large pent-up demand for consumer goods among the civilian population and a large amount of cash available to returning soldiers, suggesting that the economy would thrive. That proved to be the case. A slightly more developed model later correctly predicted that there would be only a modest recession following the Korean War, while many other economists were again predicting depression.

Over a dozen major firms now provide econometric modeling services, and some have been providing quarterly estimates for over 20 years. These services are purchased by industrial corporations, financial firms, government offices (federal, state, local, and international), and foreign companies. Moreover, many models have been developed for foreign countries, and efforts are under way (through Project LINK, sponsored by the Social Science Research Council) to create a model of the world trade system by integrating macroeconomic models of the economies of individual countries and regions, including some eastern European countries. Efforts are just beginning to be made to incorporate the People's Republic of China into a world model.

These developments have depended heavily on basic research on macroeconomic processes, and almost all of the developmental work necessary to create the models—the theory of system design, the methods of estimation, the methods of testing, the techniques of simulation, and data management procedures—has been done in economics departments and research centers of universities.

Related Developments

Modern production methods taught in business schools are the direct outgrowth of optimization theory developed through basic research in economics. Linear programming, scheduling theory, inventory control theory, quality control models, production forecasting models, etc., used extensively by businesses, the military, and almost all other large organizations, are all the direct descendants of yesterday's basic research in economics. But production is not the only area of business that has been profoundly affected by basic research. Modern finance and accounting both reflect the theory of decision making under uncertainty that was a major academic innovation a few years back. And portfolio management techniques have revolutionized the operations of banks and related financial institutions.

CHANGES IN THE WAY WE DO THINGS

Concrete applications of findings from basic research in the behavioral and social sciences can be divided into two main categories: those concerned with human performance or the design of human environments and those concerned with the structuring of social, economic, and political systems. The former category mainly includes applications of psychological theory and research, principally psychophysics and learning theory. The latter category encompasses organizational analysis, applications of location theory, economic and demographic analysis, and the evaluation of economic and social programs, among others. Many of the latter applications involve the identification and analysis of problems rather than the creation of solutions. This is because most issues having to do with social and economic arrangements do not admit of technical solutions; they require instead political solutions, that is, adjudication among competing interests and conflicting values. The role of research in this context is to provide the framework within which debate can proceed, by identifying the issues involved and providing the information necessary for their resolution.

In this section we review a few examples from both of these categories. Again, our examples are illustrative; we have made no attempt to be comprehensive.

HUMAN FACTORS APPLICATIONS

Human factors engineering is a branch of technology that is concerned with the application of theoretical and experimental psychology to human-machine systems. There are vast numbers of such systems, the designs of which can be judiciously directed by the results of cognitive research. For example, how should a control panel be designed so that the operator can most easily remember the operation of numerous dials and switches? The poor design of the instrument panel at Three Mile Island has been said to have been an important contributor to the accident there. How should aircraft instrument panels be designed so that pilots can efficiently monitor them, operate controls, and follow complicated instructions from a ground controller, often simultaneously? Basic research has shown that information from a large number of sources (for example, the instruments on an aircraft) is both more easily acquired and more resistant to being forgotten if the information is initially organized in some coherent manner (Nelson and Smith, 1972). It therefore makes sense to group the instruments according to their inherent hierarchical structure. A pilot scanning the panel is then making use of the inherent organization of the information that he is trying to acquire and remember.

In a similar way, research on memory has been applied in the design of a variety of codes and classifications, such as telephone numbers and industrial inventory codes. And research on color and shape perception and on stimulus complexity has been used to design identification codes that minimize sorting and processing errors.

Basic research in psychophysics (for a review of this field see the paper by Braida et al. in Part II) has been applied to a variety of problems, including the design of alarm systems based on knowledge of how people perceive and process information; the design of devices to aid the handicapped, such as reading machines for the blind; the design of tools and workplaces based on an understanding of human capabilities; the redesign of aircraft engines to eliminate sound frequencies shown to be irritating to crew and passengers; and the decision about how much pigment to put in pavement markers.

One particularly interesting example is the identification of visual illusions in night landing situations as the cause of certain airplane accidents (Kraft, 1978). In the year the Boeing 727 jetliner was introduced, there were four crashes in which the plane landed short of the runway. The first suspicion was that there was a design flaw in the aircraft. However, an analysis of the accidents revealed that all four had occurred at night, when the aircraft was being flown under visual (as opposed to instrument) flight rules, and all four occurred in locations in which the approach included a "dark hole" (a body of water or uninhabited desert) with city lights visible beyond the airport. Examination of the records of other accidents revealed that a large fraction occurred under similar circumstances. This observation led to the hypothesis that accidents occurred as the result of a visual illusion that caused the pilot to believe that the aircraft was at a higher altitude than it actually was. The hypothesis was confirmed by a series of experiments using a flight simulator. A simple remedy was available and was implemented: Pilots were made aware of the visual illusion and encouraged to monitor their altimeters frequently during night visual approaches. By changing standard cockpit procedures—requiring the copilot to call out altimeter readings—the problem of accidents due to overestimating altitude has been virtually eliminated.

APPLICATIONS OF LEARNING THEORY

An important area of basic research in psychology has been the study of how organisms learn, and a particularly important approach to this topic has been through the principles derived from classical conditioning and instrumental learning experiments (Kimble, 1968). The main idea in classical conditioning, associated mainly with the work of Pavlov, is that of the *conditioned response*. Pavlov's best-known experiment consisted of exposing a dog simultaneously to both food and a neutral stimulus—a light, buzzer, bell, or ticking metronome. The inherent response of dogs to food is salivation. Pavlov's crucial discovery was that, by associating food with the neutral stimulus for several trials, he could train or condition dogs to salivate in response to the neutral stimulus in the absence of food. Subsequently it has been demonstrated that a wide range of responses may be conditioned in the same way, including galvanic skin response, eye blinks, a blocking of the alpha rhythm of the brain, pupil dilation, vasodilation, vasoconstriction, and the secretions from various internal organs.

The main idea in instrumental learning is that organisms increase behavior that is rewarded—that is, they learn to do what is rewarded. A great deal of research has gone into the experimental investigation and elaboration of this simple idea, to determine under what conditions and at what rate learning is likely to take place and to specify aspects of the learning process. Principles of learning apply to many species, not just humans.

Therapeutic Applications

Although initiated and developed purely to study the learning process, learning theory has proved to have great practical value. Behavior modification procedures based on principles of learning theory (see the paper by Wilson in Part II) have proved highly successful in the treatment of phobias and fears. They have also revolutionized the treatment of severely disturbed long-term schizophrenic patients in mental hospitals through the development of token economies in which desirable behavior is rewarded by tokens that can be exchanged for privileges and goods (Ayllon and Azrin, 1968). The results of such efforts have been dramatic, radically improving the level of functioning of severely disturbed schizophrenic patients.

A different use of learning theory principles is the development of biofeedback procedures for the control of autonomic nervous system responses, such as heart rate, blood pressure, and skin temperature. It has recently been discovered, contrary to conventional wisdom, that such responses can be controlled by individuals when feedback is provided by means of electronic monitoring instruments; the feedback itself serves as a reinforcer (reward), leading to the learned control of the physiological response. These procedures, still in the experimental stage, promise considerable therapeutic benefit for coping with such disorders as high blood pressure, migraine headaches, seizure disorders, sexual dysfunctions, and muscular paralysis (see the paper by Krantz et al. in Part II).

Pedagogical Applications

An early application of learning theory to pedagogy was Thorndike's development of drill methods for teaching basic arithmetic and spelling skills, which dominated elementary school curricula for many years (National Research Council, 1981:158). More recently, the development of computer-aided instruction has been strongly influenced by cognitive psychologists who saw the possibility of implementing modern learning theories through the use of computer-aided management of individual instructional routines. This form of instruction is still experimental with regard to its mass application in schools, but it is now widely used in specialized training in industrial settings. Another area of great promise is the application of cognitive principles to the teaching of reading (see the paper by Carpenter and Just in Part II for a review of current developments).

Other Applications

Although it does not involve human subjects, one particularly interesting application of classical conditioning that illustrates the underlying principles involved is the conditioning of taste to control predators (Gustavson et al., 1974, 1976; Ellins et al., 1977). Experimenters in California have been salting sheep ranges frequented by coyotes with mutton laced with lithium chloride, which produces violent illness. Coyotes that have become ill though lithium chloride poisoning cease entirely their attacks on sheep; one exposure to laced mutton is sufficient. Conditioned coyotes prey on grain-eating and plague-carrying rodents, thus controlling another troublesome pest population. Estimates of savings in lost stock run in the millions of dollars.

Like many other practical applications, predator control was accomplished by exploiting basic research from several areas—not only learning theory but also a great deal of basic research on the psychophysiology of taste that was carried out with no expectation of possible applications. As with other applications, this first success has led to attempts to generalize it to other contexts.

Organizational Analysis

The use of basic research to improve the design of formal organizations and other social institutions has not been as systematic or as comprehensive as the exploitation of basic research on learning, cognition, and perception has been for human engineering improvements. Rather, as the examples reviewed below show, the main function of the research has been to illuminate areas of potential difficulty and hence to caution managers about the complexity of the decisions they have to make.

Organizations and Management

Research on formal organizations has thus far not led to the discovery of a set of general principles that can be uniformly applied to the solution of concrete organizational problems. That is not to say that organizational analysts have no useful function, but rather that research findings have served to provide insights and leads to solutions rather than direct design prescriptions. Organizational design thus remains something of an art, depending heavily on the analyst's perceptiveness and ability to translate research findings from one organizational context to another. However, fundamental research can illuminate managerial options and allow somewhat more informed managerial judgments to be made. This process can be illustrated by considering some ways in which research on ambiguity and loose coupling in organizations has led to an improved awareness of some possible traps in managing hierarchical organizations. These managerial implications are incidental to the original research, which was designed to understand how organizations behave, particularly how they make and implement decisions, not to discover ways of improving that behavior.

Several recent studies have observed that formal organizations frequently exhibit loose coupling between problems and solutions, between decision processes and decision outcomes, between different parts of an organization, between policies and implementation, and between action taken today and action taken yesterday. At the same time, it has been observed that organizations frequently act with imprecise or ambiguous goals, that they make inferences about the world on the basis of ambiguous information, and that they often exhibit considerable unresolved internal conflict. In terms of conventional management theory, it is natural to see such phenomena as symptomatic of organizational inadequacies. Sometimes they are. However, these apparently anomalous behaviors are often sensible.

One example: It seems to be true that organizations often adapt better to highly uncertain or rapidly changing situations if they are organized in a decentralized and loosely coupled way. Yet, as Perrow (1980) observes in his organizational analysis of Three Mile Island, administrative propensities often lead to centralizing control in a crisis. Such propensities may be appropriate in some situations (e.g., the Cuban missile crisis), but people at the top of an organization are likely to exaggerate the gains from centralized crisis management and underestimate the losses.

A second example: Although hierarchical organizations require effective managerial control, they also require some slack—some unexploited opportunities, irrelevant activities, and loose management. Slack provides a buffer against environmental uncertainties (including competition). In effect, it is a way for organizations to transfer resources (including opportunities) from good times to bad. At the same time, slack encourages and permits subunit and individual deviation from current organizational plans, priorities, and preferences. This "foolishness" is hard to justify in terms of calculated optimality, but it is a source of innovation and change. Not yet understood, however, are the optimal mixture of structure and slack and the conditions under which the optimal balance may vary.

A third example: Although it is clear that precision in objectives often produces benefits for organizations, managerial maxims seem to underestimate the associated costs. In particular, precise performance measures encourage organizational participants to discover ways to score well without necessarily doing well. For example, the orientation to short-run profits or goals characteristic of many business organizations in the United States often has the apparent consequence of stimulating managers to manage accounts (e.g., profit and loss statements, stock evaluations) rather than technologies and products. The long-run health of the organization is thus sacrificed to short-run cleverness. This kind of goal displacement is a common consequence of the attempt to formulate objectives in concrete terms. Another classic example is the tendency of students to focus their studies on what will be covered on the final examination, not on what is required to master a subject.

Japanese Management

Students of industrial productivity have in recent years become increasingly interested in understanding the ways in which Japanese firms are managed. Their interest stems from the obvious success of contemporary Japanese firms in developing and marketing superior products in a profitable way in several major industries that were once viewed as primarily American domains— e.g., steel, automobiles, and electronics. Japanese industrial successes, and American declines, have been attributed to many things, among them the ways in which firms in the two countries deal with employees, organize quality control, and make managerial decisions. Some conspicuous features of Japanese management procedures (e.g., quality control circles) have been proposed for imitation in American firms and have been selectively adopted.

This openness to borrowing parallels an earlier Japanese enthusiasm for learning from American experience in management, but with a difference. Contemporary American approaches to Japanese management tend to focus on specific techniques or practices that could be copied. The discussions have not been in all cases sufficiently thoughtful and critical. Elementary cautions about the many ways in which Japanese experience reflects a profoundly different technological, social, and historical setting seem often to be ignored (Cole, 1980). There needs to be, for example, more effort to relate the specific Japanese aspects of worker involvement to research on participation, decentralization, and alienation and less reliance on casual and selective observations about Japanese management and how it works.

Japanese fascination with American management was somewhat more systematic. In particular, it apparently entailed less concern with specific techniques and more concern with research on organizations. Japanese emphases on quality control, on worker involvement in developing and implementing quality improvement, and on team concepts of work were refined by detailed consideration of basic research on organizations. For the most part the Japanese strategy seems to have been to use ideas drawn from research to develop managerial practices appropriate to Japanese culture and traditions. This explicit attention to the intellectual and research foundations of management practice is reflected in the Japanese awareness of the work of American students of organizations, such as Argyris, Blau, Deming, Haire, Herzberg, Leavitt, Likert, March, McGregor, and Simon.

It is easy to exaggerate the contrast between Japanese and American instincts for cross-national learning. Part of the contrast is undoubtedly attributable more to differences between American and Japanese conventions of exposition and attribution than to differences in modes of thought. Still, some American enthusiasts for copying Japanese management neither appreciate the irony nor consistently recognize the risks of a style that can be likened to learning French in order to read T. S. Eliot in French translation.

RESOURCE ALLOCATION

The most basic statement of economic theory is that under certain conditions a competitive market will result in an efficient allocation of resources. Yet society uses many mechanisms other than competitive markets to allocate scarce resources, including auctions, committees, and elections. A good deal of theoretical research has been devoted to investigating how these mechanisms work. While the properties of various allocation mechanisms are among the most abstract topics in economics (see the discussion of social choice in Chapter 3), research in this area has also been among the most applicable. It has led fairly directly to proposals (some of which have been implemented) for changing the rules by which offshore oil leases are auctioned, public television licenses are awarded, and landing rights are allocated at crowded airports.

The recent major reform of regulation (e.g., airline and transportation deregulation) depended heavily on economic analysis based on modern econometric techniques. Exchange rate deregulation and brokerage fee deregulation have also involved decisions based on considerable analysis about the possible evolution of market prices and structure.

Continuing research by economists is establishing both what is efficient about free market pricing and what its limitations are. An important limitation is the "free rider" problem. Certain goods and services are freely available to everyone once they are developed. Hence it is economically rational for a given individual or firm *not* to invest in their development but to become a free rider on the return to the investments of others. These goods and services, such as environmental improvements and basic research, are known as public goods. The optimal allocation mechanism for public goods is not the market but rather public subsidies. An analogous situation occurs in the case of negative externalities, costs that are borne by parties external to those who create them (the contamination of a swimming beach by industrial waste is an example of a negative externality). Public goods, of course, involve positive externalities, benefits to those other than the creators of such goods. When either positive or negative externalities exist, unfettered competition will involve inefficiencies that could be ameliorated by regulations, taxes, and subsidies and by recognition of new forms of property rights and rights of legal redress. In the case of finite nonrenewable resources that have to be rationed for future decades, research is necessary to appraise the degree to which the free play of market pricing will yield an optimal timing of resource exploitation.

Research on externalities has had other applications as well. The structure of tort and liability law has been changing as the courts and legislatures have realized that the distribution of the burden of risk can have a major impact on the functioning of the economy. At one time manufacturers could shift to the consumer the risk of injury due to a faulty product design and further avoid liability by operating through a retailer. The fact that firms now must assume this risk has dramatically affected the nature of the business-consumer relationship. The considerations that led to this change can be traced directly to the basic research of the 1960s. This same body of research has profoundly affected other fields of law, such as tax law, antitrust law, and public utility regulation.

Microeconomic research, based on the Panel Study of Income Dynamics, supported by the National Science Foundation (which has followed 5,000 families for 14 years, yielding the only reliable longitudinal data on the economic behavior of families and individuals), has provided the basis for policy decisions in several areas. A major finding of this study, which was possible only because of its longitudinal design, is that poverty is by and large a temporary rather than a permanent condition. Rather than a sizable underclass perpetuating a "culture of poverty," the poor consist mainly of those who, through family dissolution or other events, have fallen temporarily on hard times. Lane and Morgan (1975:34), analyzing data from the first six years of the study, found that while in any given year about 10 percent of the sample had income insufficient to meet their needs, only 2 percent were in this condition all six years, and 21 percent of the sample experienced poverty in at least one of the six years. The paper by Heckman and Michael (in Part II) reviews related outcomes of microeconomic research.

LOCATIONAL ANALYSIS

Basic research by geographers and regional scientists on locational problems originated with a rather straightforward issue: Where would economically rational producers locate their factories, processing plants, distributional warehouses, and retail outlets relative to energy, raw materials, labor supply, and markets to maintain a competitive profit position? A related question was: How can observed spatial distributions of manufacturing and farm production, labor concentrations, and transport linkages between places be accounted for? These questions were regarded as straightforward, though not simple to model, because the underlying structure of the models was based on the simplifying assumption that production and market behavior would be such as to minimize costs. Subsequent analyses provided elaborations of the basic models to yield better conformity between actual patterns and those predicted by theory. By the end of the 1960s, location theory was fairly well specified; a large variety of modeling approaches had been developed and tested, and the knowledge acquired was being put to use to locate new plants, shopping areas, transportation facilities and routes, and even towns and cities.

A number of postwar developments caught up with locational analysis by the end of the 1960s and the decade of the 1970s. Of particular importance were innovations in telecommunications, the growth of the service sector and high-technology production, and the relative decline of heavy industry dependent on proximity to bulky raw materials. In consequence, transportation costs became less important for siting decisions relative to other factors, such as the proximity of a well-trained administrative, technical, and clerical labor force, state and local tax policy, and the presence of recreational, cultural, and climatic amenities. These developments were incorporated into new models, which in their turn proved to be capable of providing reasonable predictions and general guidelines for siting decisions based on comparative cost methods.

The most profound challenge to locational analysis emerged with greater public recognition of the effects of siting decisions. Everyone cannot be equally accessible to desirable facilities, such as workplaces, bus stops, libraries, fire stations, and hospitals. Furthermore, everyone cannot be equally remote from nuclear power plants, toxic waste deposits, solid waste disposal plants, drug treatment centers, and group homes for delinquents. To take account of preferences for accessibility to or distance from desired or noxious facilities, respectively, it was necessary to elaborate the models used to determine optimal sites. In particular, normative concepts were needed for balancing the virtues of efficiency with those of equity and justice.

Analysis thus turned to the identification and measurement of neighborhood spillovers, the negative externalities that are most prominent close to a site and diminish with distance from it. To cite an example, a new hospital in a residential area displaces apartment dwellers to provide a residence for nurses. The apartment dwellers are relocated but must pay a larger share of their income for rent. The additional traffic, parking, and noise from ambulances detract from the quality of life for those who are left. The hospital serves and benefits a large portion of the city, yet its costs are borne largely by local residents. Similarly, nuclear power plants impose severe costs to land use in their immediate vicinity. Moreover, a serious accident would affect the population living within a large radius around the facility. New urban highways impose noise and some hazard to neighboring areas. Neighbors of sites selected for group homes for the mentally handicapped, delinquents, or drug abusers voice complaints about added hazards, undesired neighborhood change, and declining property values.

There has been some success in measuring these unintended neighborhood spillovers, including both tangible factors and many of the intangible ones. Comprehensive impact analyses can be carried out to evaluate alternative sites, with one option being to build no facility at all. These analyses provide the bases for assessing the true costs of projects and facilities.

Basic research applicable to the solution of these complex and controversial siting problems is not limited to location theory and welfare economics. Basic contributions in political theory have been found to be of great relevance in understanding the mechanisms of threat and conflict that are often the outcome of imposed siting solutions. The same body of literature is helpful in developing negotiation and arbitration mechanisms for involving citizen groups in the resolution of siting conflicts.

PROGRAM AND POLICY EVALUATION

Another important area of application of basic research in the social and behavioral sciences is the analysis of actual practices, programs, policies, and plans. Sometimes the analysis is retrospective, to decide what went wrong, as in the case of the Three Mile Island nuclear reactor accident. Organizational sociologists and human factors psychologists who were members of the study commission were able to identify flaws in both organizational and human factors design. This sort of analysis is quite analogous to what engineers do when a bridge falls or an airplane crashes. Often analysis is undertaken of ongoing programs or activities, to understand them better and perhaps improve them. Periodic educational assessments and management reviews are cases in point. Finally, there are analyses of proposed future courses of action or policies, to anticipate their consequences.

Procedures for analyzing specific programs have been formalized under the rubric of *evaluation research*. But even social and behavioral scientists who do not identify themselves as evaluation researchers often engage in this kind of activity. As we have noted, the analysis of alternative economic policies is a major part of the work of many economists. More and more, the work of social scientists is employed by congressional research agencies such as the Congressional Budget Office and the Office of Technology Assessment. And many basic researchers from time to time find themselves addressing quite specific problems with practical implications.

Evaluation techniques emerged directly from the development of research methods in a number of the social and behavioral sciences, in particular psychology, survey research, and economics, in which serious attention has been paid to the development of sensitive assessment methods to determine experimental outcomes in complex settings. As a result, a sophisticated set of analytic procedures has been transferred to nonacademic settings.

One particularly interesting evaluation study is that reported by Frederick Mosteller in his 1981 presidential address to the American Association for the Advancement of Science (Mosteller, 1981). He studied 28 social, medical, and technological innovations, each designed to provide some specific benefit or improve some specific outcome; in another study (Gilbert, McPeek, and Mosteller, 1977), 36 medical innovations based on randomized clinical trials were studied. In both studies, Mosteller found that only about half the innovations yielded positive benefit (most of the others had little effect and a few were actually harmful). Such findings are of crucial importance as a corrective to the all-too-frequent tendency to implement proposed innovations on the strength of their plausibility alone, a tendency especially pronounced among policy makers with respect to social innovations.

In some instances the federal government has asked social scientists for research explicitly designed to aid in the advance evaluation of public policy alternatives. A prominent example of such research is the large-scale social policy experiment. As the federal government considers major reforms in health, housing, and welfare policies, it has sponsored experimental programs to evaluate in advance the effect of potential national programs. Among these experiments have been programs for income maintenance (Heclo and Rein, 1980), health insurance (Orr, 1980), and housing subsidies (Field, 1980). Similar research projects, on a somewhat smaller scale, have assessed programs for employment training, criminal rehabilitation, and preschool education. Concepts and methods from the social sciences have been used in designing these studies, collecting the data, and interpreting the results.

A different kind of evaluation research involves the examination of an ongoing program, to decide whether to continue it or how to improve it. A case in point is the Head Start program. In the early 1960s several comprehensive reviews of psychological research suggested that early life experiences are crucial in the formation of intelligence and in comprehensive development (see especially Hunt, 1961; Bloom, 1964). This research led to the inference that children whose early life experiences were impoverished would be permanently handicapped in their cognitive development, and hence in their educational achievement, and also to the hypothesis that early intervention—in the form of intellectually stimulating and supportive pre-school experience—could give such children a head start in life that would permanently improve their intellectual performance and life chances. These ideas, developing at a time when the war on poverty was being fought through a variety of social and economic programs, led to the creation of Project Head Start, a national program of compensatory preschool education, and to a large number of similar locally based programs. Many of these programs were designed as experiments, to test whether appropriate preschool education could increase IQ and improve school performance.

The history of this research is illuminating, cautioning against premature generalization about the effects of social intervention. The first results were extremely encouraging. Several studies found a sharp increase in the IQ of children enrolled in the programs when compared with children not enrolled. However, a second round of studies came to much gloomier conclusions, finding that IQ and performance changes were often short-lived, disappearing a year or two after the children had left the program. While one interpretation attributes the latter finding to the continuing influence of school environments, noting that both the experimental and control groups tended subsequently to experience the same, largely inadequate elementary schooling, the more general interpretation was that compensatory education has no lasting effects.

This conclusion in its turn proved premature, however, as evidence began to accumulate regarding the long-term effects of early interventions. While permanent IQ changes did not in general occur, children exposed to the preschool programs were less likely to require special education, less likely to be held back in grade, and more likely to complete high school; they also tended to score somewhat better on academic achievement tests and to have higher educational aspirations (Brown and Grotberg, 1980; Schweinhart and Weikart, 1980:62-64,75-87). While data continue to be collected and the efficacy of preschool interventions continues to be debated, these interventions would not have been conceived without the large body of basic research on the effects of early childhood experience, and they could not have been evaluated without the procedures derived from the methods of experimental social psychology.

Often policy makers have neither the time, resources, nor inclination to design a study relevant to a specific policy choice. In such circumstances social scientists are frequently asked to review the relevant research literature and provide informed judgments about the implications of existing findings for the policy under consideration. This task is difficult and delicate because the criteria for generalizing from such findings are stringent. The task illustrates the importance and closeness of the relationship between policy research and the development of theory and methods within the social science disciplines. Policy scientists must combine conceptual and methodological skills from a diversity of disciplines and must organize these resources, usually within a short time, to address policy issues. Because the quality of policy research ultimately depends on the quality of the basic research skills and knowledge available, the usefulness of the policy sciences depends on the development of the social sciences more generally.

CHANGES IN THE WAY WE THINK ABOUT THINGS

As individuals and as sharers of a culture, people develop shared understandings about the world around them, including the social world and human nature. Not only do these understandings reflect basic cultural assumptions, but they may also be shaped and transformed by systematic knowledge. In the United States empirically based and verified knowledge recently has come to play an important role in shaping our society's understanding of itself and of human nature. The consequence has been a fundamental transformation in the way we think about ourselves and our social arrangements. Most obviously, human behavior and social structure are now widely perceived as orderly, explicable, and amenable to systematic empirical investigation. Moreover, social and behavioral research has dramatically altered the understanding of the informed public regarding a host of social phenomena, and it promises to continue to do so. For purposes of illustration, consider how our conceptions of race and ethnicity and their correlates and our understanding of unemployment have changed as a result of social and behavioral research.

THE CHANGING CONCEPTION OF RACE AND ETHNICITY

The transformation of conventional wisdom on the nature of race and ethnicity over the course of this century can readily be traced through a comparison of successive editions of the *Encyclopaedia Britannica*. The 11th edition, published in 1911 and purported to be a comprehensive summary of available knowledge (Koning, 1981), was quite clear in its conclusions about "the Negro race" (in the 11th edition the world's population is divided into three distinct races; article on "Negro," p. 344):

In certain . . . characteristics . . . the negro would appear to stand on a lower evolutionary plane than the white man, and to be more closely related to the highest anthropoids. . . .

Mentally, the negro is inferior to the white. The remark of F. Manetta, made after a long study of the negro in America, may be taken as generally true of the whole race: "The negro children were sharp, intelligent, and full of vivacity, but on approaching the adult period a gradual change set in. The intellect seemed to become clouded, animation giving place to a sort of lethargy, briskness yielding to indolence. We must necessarily suppose that the development of the negro and white proceeds on different lines. While with the latter the volume of the brain grows with the expansion of the brainpan, in the former the growth of the brain is on the contrary arrested by the premature closing of the cranial sutures and lateral pressure of the frontal bone." This explanation is reasonable and even probable as a contributing cause; but evidence is lacking on the subject and the arrest or even deterioration in mental development is no doubt very largely due to the fact that after puberty sexual matters take the first place in the negro's life and thoughts.

By the 14th edition, published in 1929, the inherent mental inferiority of Negroes had come into question, although the comment about their standing on a lower evolutionary plane was retained. Carr-Sanders is quoted as concluding that "there seems to be no marked difference in innate intellectual power. The differences are rather differences in disposition and temperament, . . ." and the judgment is offered that "given suitable training, the Negro is capable of becoming a craftsman of considerable skill, particularly in metal work, carpentry and carving" (article on "Negro," p. 193). The article on "Differential Psychology" observes (p. 368) that "the inferiority of the negro to the white in mental capacity has often been asserted as the result of comparative studies, but it is difficult to say how much of the difference found is due to native against cultural factors"; it then goes on to note that "the greater the admixture of white blood, the closer does the negro approach the white in performance. . . ." The 1929 edition is agnostic on the question of racial differences in character, noting that "whether in the final analysis there is . . . a greater tendency toward crime inherent in the Negro race is a question upon which there is great difference of opinion and little scientific data" (article on "Negro, the American," p. 196).

By the publication of the 15th edition in 1974, a dramatic transformation had taken place. There is no article on "Negroes," and the article on "Minorities and Ethnic Groups" is an analysis of the social structuring of ethnic relations and the behavior of ethnic groups in multiethnic societies. On the question of racial differences in intelligence, differences in test scores are acknowledged as typical but are discounted as almost certainly a reflection of environmental differences. It is worthwhile quoting the relevant paragraphs of the article on "Intelligence, Distribution of" (pp. 676-677):

In studies of racial differences in intelligence in countries where white culture is dominant, it has been a very consistent finding that groups classified as Negro or black are likely to achieve lower scores on standard intelligence tests than do groups of whites or Caucasians. Yet, despite typically significant differences between the mean scores of the two so-called racial groups, the ranges (i.e., the spread between the lowest score and the highest score in each group) are usually found to be about the same, revealing extensive overlap in the score distributions of the two groups. Indeed, even in studies in which average scores strongly seemed to favour whites, considerable numbers of black subjects achieved higher scores than those of the average white.

Such studies have been sharply criticized since in most of them all subjects were tested by white examiners. In studies made to assess the effect of the examiner's race on the subject's scores, black children tended to earn higher scores when they were tested by black examiners than when they were tested by whites. Examiner effects should be controlled in seeking to discover possible racial differences in intelligence test scores; otherwise the results are likely to be misleading.

Black children in Northern cities of the U.S. tend to exhibit higher IQs than do black children in Southern cities; the scores achieved by Northern black children who have migrated from the South tend to increase with the length of time they have lived in the North. Controlling for such influences serves to diminish apparent racial differences considerably. Yet, when tests designed to be relatively free of cultural and language biases are used, smaller racial-group differences appear. Such differences still may reflect environmental effects upon the development of the skills necessary to achieve high scores on intelligence tests, since representation of blacks in the lower social strata throughout U.S. society in the 1970s was disproportionately large.

Thus, while it has been argued that IQ data constitute support for those theories of genetic racial inferiority, it seems more likely that the differences reflect persistent social and economic discrimination. Under legal or de facto segregation in many countries, educational facilities for blacks rarely have been equal to those provided for whites (e.g., South Africa, Angola). There is considerable evidence that the growth of intelligence, as reflected in the IQ, is influenced significantly by the quality of available educational resources regardless of race. For example, lower class whites also show lower average IQ scores than do middle class whites in European and North American countries.

How can we account for these changes in perspective? While many forces were involved, it is fair to say that research on racial differences and institutions was a significant contributor. First, many studies have been done showing that racial differences in achievements can largely be explained by differences in opportunities and environments. Perhaps the classic study in this genre is Klineberg's (1935) demonstration that while Northern whites had higher average aptitude scores than Northern blacks and Southern whites had higher average scores than Southern blacks, Northern blacks scored higher on the average than Southern whites. There have been many subsequent studies of a similar type, some mentioned in the passage from the 1974 edition of the *Encyclopaedia Britannica* quoted above. Much of this material was cited by the Supreme Court in its 1954 decision declaring separate schooling for blacks unconstitutional. Work of this kind continues today.

Second, our racial institutions have been subject to careful scrutiny by social scientists. The classic study is that by the Swedish sociologist Gunnar Myrdal, who was invited by the Carnegie Corporation in 1937 to head a comprehensive study of the race problem in America. Perhaps because Myrdal was a distinguished foreign social scientist deliberately chosen to provide an outsider's perspective, and perhaps also because he was able to enlist the aid and support of the bulk of American social scientists doing research on race relations and on the black population, his 1944 report, *An American Dilemma*, was extremely influential. This massive volume (1,483 pages) provided a comprehensive review of the social, economic, and political status of Negroes in the United States. But its real impact was due to the position it took regarding the cause of the inferior status of blacks—that it was not the peculiarities of blacks themselves that explained their position, but the history and continuing presence of discrimination against them by the white majority. The "dilemma" of the title was the discrepancy between American ideals of fairness, justice, and equality of opportunity and the reality of the treatment of the Negro minority. This report stands as a hallmark of the kind of contribution social research can make to societal self-awareness.

Third, we can now monitor changes in both racial differences and racial attitudes, thanks to the development of statistical time series. We know, for example, both that the objective position of blacks relative to whites has improved substantially in the past 40 years, with a reduction—but not complete elimination—of the gap in educational attainment, occupational achievement, and income (Farley, 1977), and that white prejudice against blacks has been markedly reduced (for example, the proportion of whites who thought blacks are as intelligent as whites rose from 40 percent in the mid-1940s to 80 percent by the early 1960s; Hyman and Sheatsley, 1964:6). An argument can be made that the very revelation of attitudes such as a belief in the inferiority of blacks contributes to their reduction, through the process of publicly labeling them as prejudices, especially when combined with a growing scientific literature attributing race differences to features of the social environment.

Finally, it has come to be recognized, through the work of both cultural anthropologists and social psychologists, that the concepts of race and ethnic group are themselves socially structured. Racial and ethnic distinctions have little or nothing to do with genetic differences but rather are social categories invoked as the basis of group identity and group differentiation. The kinds of racial or ethnic distinctions invoked and their salience vary according to historical circumstance and social setting. The Black Power movement and the subsequent resurgence of white ethnic identification, for example, are explicable as manifestations of intergroup competition for limited resources.

Equally dramatic alterations of cultural conceptions resulting from research in the behavioral and social sciences could be documented for child development, aging, sex differences in behavior, mental illness, alcoholism, and the nature of foreigners and foreign cultures. It is fair to say that as a result of such research Americans today have a very different view of human behavior and social institutions than their parents did a generation ago.

THE FUNCTION OF SOCIAL SCIENCE LABELING

The labeling process has been one of social science's most useful functions. Social scientists need to label human activities, processes, or events so that they can bound and isolate their subject for study. The public, too, needs to be able to fix human affairs by labeling them in order to examine an issue from many sides and to consider it in detachment from its ongoing, often controversial, context. By identifying issues and highlighting their most generalizable, salient features by giving them names, social scientists assist the public in thinking through its position on alternative solutions to social problems. A case in point is juvenile delinquency. The label itself identifies the phenomenon as something different from adult crime and suggests that it may have different causes and different solutions. Similarly, inflation— the reduction in the value of money—is conventionally thought of as a concomitant of rapid expansion of the economy. The term *stagflation* was invented to describe a different and new phenomenon—the reduction in the value of money in a stagnating economy. Again, the term itself suggests the need to look for causes and cures other than those conventionally associated with inflation.

Sometimes efforts to reconceptualize by redesignating go awry, as new concepts repeatedly regain their unwanted, usually negative, meanings. Consider the search for appropriate ways to categorize societies that have not attained the levels of commercial and industrial development of the modern West. Over the past century social thinkers and social scientists have used a succession of terms for these societies—*savage, primitive, backward, nonliterate, preliterate, undeveloped, underdeveloped, less developed, developing*, and finally, in a kind of desperation, simply *new*—only to find each term picking up connotations of inferiority. We have also had trouble referring to the very poor in society, seeking euphemisms like the *hard-to-reach* and *problem families*, only to find these labels failing as well. From these examples it is evident that labels are useful and tend to gain currency when they illuminate rather than obscure the phenomenon or the category they refer to (Matza, 1966).

Today our language is full of social science labels, terms whose meanings have moved from the common language to social science, which then have returned to ordinary use bearing the special meanings that social science has fixed them with. A short list of such words might include: *depression, inflation, human capital, the hidden economy, unconscious, reference group, status, standard of living, quality of life, sample, acculturation, socialization, alienation*, and *unemployment*.

To illustrate the dynamics of labeling, the history of one label—that is, one concept—is an instructive example: the word *unemployment*.

Unemployment is a venerable word, first recorded in the *Oxford English Dictionary* from John Milton's use of it in *Paradise Lost*, "Other Creatures all day long Rove idle unimploid, and less need rest." Throughout the colonial period and the early national years of the United States, the word meant something not being put to use, idle. For a spindle or a plow to be idle thus meant at most waste, but when idleness was applied to people it carried strong moral overtones. For the Puritans idle hands were the devil's playground ("For Satan finds some mischief still for idle hands to do," Isaac Watts, *Against Idleness and Mischief*), and for 19th-century Americans idleness was a potent sign of moral weakness. As a consequence a great deal of blaming of the victim attended the frequent depressions of the 19th and early 20th centuries when thousands of working men and women were thrown off their jobs and were unable to find alternative employment.

In a nation of farmers there was no lack of work to be done on the farm. In time, however, we became a nation of cities, factories, and large businesses and, consequently, of financial panics and market collapses, bread lines, throngs of men at the factory gates, and idlers and loungers on the porches and sidewalks of the cities. Despite such scenes, the popular notion that unemployment was self-chosen idleness and moral laxity foreclosed successful public debate over possible remedies for widespread suffering. What was needed in the 19th and early 20th centuries was some way to separate the personal condition of idleness from the social condition of market-induced unemployment.

Social science contributed to that separation. Economists, social reformers, sociologists, and others began in the late 19th century to use the term *unemployment* in what we would now call descriptions of labor markets and in connection with new fields, such as the study of business cycles and monetary fluctuations. As the 20th century progressed, these technical meanings of unemployment—lack of work caused by fluctuations in the demand for labor—attached to the old word, and it became possible to debate employment policies. Concurrently, as research advanced in the field, ancillary terms, like *full employment*, were coined. Indeed, so defined, full employment became a possible goal for public policy: In 1946 the United States Congress passed its first Full Employment Act.

Now that the social science meanings have become firmly affixed to the term *unemployment*, it is possible to look back to see the consequences of this redefinition of the term.

First, a large number of Americans have been liberated from undeserved stereotyping and abuse, as people have increasingly come to distinguish between large-scale social and economic events that create unemployment and the individual choice of idleness.

Second, social science knowledge about employment and unemployment has led to new questions, new subjects, and the coining of new words. The simple questions of when is a person unemployed and how unemployment is to be measured have turned out to be immensely complex social and economic subjects. For example, before the Great Depression of the 1930s, government statistics on the work force were maintained on the number of people with a gainful occupation. But with this approach it was not possible to make a satisfactory count of the number of people who wished to work but could not find jobs. To fashion policy during the 1930s, the government needed a count of the number of people seeking jobs. The concept of *gainfully employed* was replaced by a new concept, the *labor force*, which included everyone in the population age 14 and older (later 16 and older) who, during a specified period (usually the week prior to the date of data collection), actually had a job or was seeking work for pay. Thus the working-age population could be divided into those with a job, those unemployed and seeking work, and those not in the labor force (retired, keeping house, going to school, institutionalized, etc.). This concept has guided the collection of labor market statistics ever since. Not only has it permitted the monitoring of the unemployment rate (which is now done on a monthly basis by the U.S. Bureau of Labor Statistics using data from the Current Population

Survey, a sample survey conducted by the U.S. Bureau of the Census) but it has also provided better estimates of labor force participation rates for various demographic groups. Of great interest is the long-term trend toward a convergence of the levels of labor force participation of men and women: The rate for women is increasing and is now over 50 percent, while that for men is declining and is now about 75 percent.

Research in the 1980s suggests there is a need to adjust economic and demographic statistical series again. Social scientists are now documenting the existence and apparent permanence of an informal economy and system of production. Some estimates, for example, suggest that unreported income could amount to 10 percent of the gross national product in the United States and even more in other countries, such as Italy. Research on the informal labor market helps to clarify patterns of intranational and international labor migration. It casts issues of unemployment in a new and sharper light. It also raises questions about the accuracy of national measures of economic growth and productivity. Recent evidence indicates an explosive growh in employment in the service and light manufacturing sectors, much of it hidden from the present accounting system (for a review see Ginzberg and Vojta, 1981). It is research of this sort that can lead to a reconception and improvement of the national reporting system.

Finally, the multiplicity of social science meanings that attach to the word *unemployment* as research proceeds does not foreclose, but rather informs, public debate about employment and unemployment. Should mothers of infants work outside the home for wages? If they work part time, or if they quit for two years and then seek to return to paid work, are they unemployed? Should teenagers be working? Are they, in the language of the 17th century, idle ''great boys'' who are liable to become rogues and vagabonds? Should families be coaxed or coerced into moving from regions of high unemployment to regions of plentiful jobs? Such questions all gain accuracy and concreteness from social science research, but none can be answered except by reference to public values and the political process.

5 The National Interest in the Support of Basic Research

CONCLUSIONS

In the committee's judgment, the evidence surveyed in the previous chapters on research advances in the behavioral and social sciences and the range of uses to which such advances have been put leads to a single, fundamental conclusion: Basic research in the behavioral and social sciences is a national resource that should be sustained and encouraged through public support. Federal investment in basic research in the behavioral and social sciences, like investment in other branches of science, is an investment in the future welfare of the nation. Supporting this conclusion are a number of considerations.

(1) *Basic research in the behavioral and social sciences has yielded an impressive array of accomplishments, and there is every reason to expect the yield from future research to be at least as great.* At an accelerating rate during recent decades, such research has been responsible for (a) greatly increased substantive knowledge of individual behavior, social institutions, and cultural patterns under a wide variety of changing as well as stable conditions; (b) markedly improved methods of data collection and analysis, which have not only led to new discoveries and the resolution of old debates but also have provided the foundation for information technologies (e.g., sample surveys, standardized tests, economic indicators) now regarded as indispensable in the public and private sectors; and (c) continuing development of pedagogical and therapeutic procedures, of devices and arrangements for improving human performance and the human environment, and of procedures

93

for evaluating public policies and proposed programs. Some of these developments are reviewed in the preceding two chapters and the papers accompanying this report; many others could be cited as well. On the basis of these kinds of contributions, the behavioral and social sciences merit support.

(2) *The benefits of basic research are seldom if ever predictable in advance; they are often unanticipated and still more often the outcome of complex, discontinuous sequences of discovery, insight, and invention. Investment in basic research must be regarded as investment in a process that is expected to yield substantial contributions to individual and social well-being, but it cannot be regarded as a direct purchase of those contributions.* There are several reasons for this.

First, it is generally not clear in advance where or when major scientific discoveries or breakthroughs will occur. The history of research in all fields is one of unforeseen interpenetrations of findings, insights, and methodological advances, false starts, miscues, and provisional answers later superseded by superior formulations. Sequences of steps that, with hindsight, seem to constitute a consistent advance toward a particular goal often were experienced by those responsible for them as confused, accidental, and haphazard. Similarly, rates of progress are seldom predictable to those immediately involved. Although cumulative over the long run, the orderliness of scientific research generally emerges only in retrospect. Hence it generally is not possible to identify specific areas or topics as targets for special attention or intensive support with any confidence that they and not some other area will yield major new insights or discoveries.

Second, specific research findings rarely translate automatically or directly to any particular use or application. Once it is published, scientific knowledge becomes available for any and all possible applications. A common—and indeed highly desirable—fate is that a particular finding will be utilized in ways never even imagined by its discoverers. And, conversely, a given application typically will exploit findings, methods, and procedures from a wide variety of disciplines and research areas, often in a long and complex chain of development.

An attempt to trace the research and development underlying 10 major clinical advances in medicine and surgery (between 1945 and 1975) confirms this view. On the basis of a thorough review of the research literature, Comroe and Dripps (1977) identified 663 articles that they regarded as essential for one or more of the advances. Four points are of special interest. First, more than 40 percent of the articles "reported research done by scientists whose goal at that time was *unrelated* to the later clinical advance. . . . Such unrelated research was often unexpected, unpredictable, and usually greatly accelerated advance in many fields" (Comroe and Dripps, 1977:2).

Second, each of the clinical advances depended on the cumulation of dozens of studies conducted by hundreds of investigators; no advance could be attributed to the work of a single researcher or a single research group. Third, the lag between an initial discovery and its effective clinical application was usually substantial: Of 111 discoveries investigated, 57 percent had been applied more than 20 years after publication. Finally, the 663 articles identified as essential contributions were culled from a review of more than 6,000 published articles. It is highly improbable that "essential contributions" could have been identified in advance, especially given the typical long lag before application.

These findings provide firm support for the conclusion that basic research must be encouraged without regard for its immediate applicability. While we do not know from the study just described what fraction of basic research eventually comes to be applied, we do know that, in the biomedical field at least, clinical (that is, applied) advances depend heavily on basic research efforts, that it takes a great deal of research to produce each "essential contribution," and that it is impossible to predict in advance which contributions will prove essential. Moreover, applications are often very slow in coming; hence a demand for short-run payoff would be shortsighted indeed.

While parallel research in the behavioral and social sciences has not yet been conducted, the process described by Comroe and Dripps for the biomedical sciences is probably applicable to them as well.[1] Certainly, most of the applications mentioned in the previous chapter have drawn on basic

---

[1]This process probably differs, moreover, from that reported in a study entitled "Project Hindsight," conducted some years ago by the Department of Defense. That study, in attempting to track the sources of the scientific and technological innovations that were employed in new or improved weapons systems, reached the conclusion that only a small fraction of one percent of them came from "undirected science." The study concluded, more sweepingly, that "it is unusual for random, disconnected fragments of scientific knowledge to find application rapidly. It is, rather, the evaluated, compressed, organized, interpreted, and simplified scientific knowledge that we find to be the most effective connection between the undirected research laboratory and the world of practical affairs" (Sherwin and Isenson, 1967:1577). We suggest that this conclusion might have arisen from the circumstance that the investigators were looking backward from the limited perspective of a single weapons system. Different conclusions might have emerged if they had traced forward projections from a new and fundamental idea, identifying its combinations and recombinations with other ideas, findings, and methods, to its ultimate applications. In addition, Project Hindsight gave no consideration to scientific contributions that might have occurred more than 20 years prior to the final completion of the weapons systems chosen for study, thus possibly passing over basic scientific studies that contributed to the foundation for later applications. It is quite possible that the basic physical, ballistic, and electronic principles that underlie weapons design were established much earlier. If 57 percent of the essential contributions to clinical advances in medicine were made more than 20 years before their application, the percentage is likely to be far higher with respect to weapons systems.

research developments in a variety of disciplines, as have many of the applications mentioned in the papers.

(3) *The coupling between basic research in the behavioral and social sciences and its applications to public policy is significant and growing, but it is also inherently loose, uncertain, incomplete, and often slow.* Policies are properly constrained by political, social, and cultural considerations that may change in importance. To apply similar constraints to basic research would limit its effectiveness as a long-term source of new insights and approaches needed to meet unanticipated conditions. The health and vitality of scientific investigations require that at times they probe into areas of deeply held beliefs about human nature and the world. Research on the origins of the universe, on the evolution of life, on recombinant DNA, and on the heritability of traits can have this quality. In the behavioral and social sciences, that quality sometimes can apply to human evolution, to the mutually supporting or opposing influences of families, communities, and government agencies on individual development and economic well-being, and to many areas of deviance and unconventional or asocial behavior. Hence any direct transmission of findings is hindered by the differences between contexts in which scientific knowledge is generated and consumed. If the primary purpose of basic research were to effect social change or reform, it would be a frustratingly unpredictable and at best marginally effective way to achieve that end. But what identifies research as basic is for the most part a fundamentally different motivation—the concern to understand and explain human behavior and the consequences of social arrangements.

Moreover, public policy decisions in all areas, including those involving scientific and technical considerations, are made and implemented through a political process rather than by means of strictly technical judgments. Decisions involve considerations that are not resolvable on technical grounds, such as individual and group values, ideological stances, and tolerance for risk and uncertainty. While expert advice and technical judgments may make an important contribution, public choices depend primarily on a balancing of short-run and long-run considerations as to the deployment of scarce resources that are worked out in compromise among cooperating, competing, and conflicting interests. This is true of policies affecting the location of dams and nuclear power plants, the provision of artificial kidney machines, and the choice of weapons systems as well as decisions regarding fiscal policy, crime control, school desegregation, and remedial reading. The persistence of disturbingly high (although possibly declining) inflation rates should not be regarded as a failure of economics, nor crime in the streets as a failure of sociology, nor venereal disease as a failure of medicine, nor the medfly invasion of California as a failure of entomology, nor the nuclear arms race as a failure of physics. Each case mentioned is the consequence of a myriad of factors, only some of which are amenable to scientific or technical resolution.

Especially great difficulties in applying empirical knowledge to purposive action can arise when there is lack of consensus on what constitutes a problem or what solutions are acceptable. In many areas connected with health, there is widespread acceptance of the social values in question. One of the reasons that applications such as the Salk vaccine program are relatively uncontroversial is that there is a basic consensus supporting innovations to improve health; the only issues involved are technical ones regarding the efficacy and safety of alternative vaccines. But that is not always the case. When such consensus breaks down, as it has with respect to abortion, technical knowledge is no longer a sufficient basis for action. Issues regarding what kinds of knowledge from the social and behavioral sciences are felt to be pertinent often entail a similar lack of consensus. The case of poverty was noted in the previous chapter. Is it strictly an economic condition resulting from major social malfunctions, so that those caught up in it deserve every assistance as they strive to escape? Or is it also a set of self-reinforcing attitudes and behaviors with negative moral overtones that society should seek ways to modify? Both the definition of the problem itself and appropriate solutions depend on one's value position along a wide spectrum of possibilities between these polar positions.

Finally, many social policies have multiple, sometimes unanticipated consequences, so that the effort to solve one problem may simply exacerbate others. For example, efforts to improve the educational opportunities of minority children through school desegregation may have resulted in some instances in increased residential segregation as a result of "white flight" beyond the boundaries of school districts. In a complex society in which people are free to act in their own interests, as best they perceive them, the translation of knowledge from the social sciences into the solution of social problems is likely to be particularly difficult.

Despite this, there is evidence that basic research in the social and behavioral sciences does have an important impact on public policy. As with other sorts of applications, the impact is long term and relatively indirect (Weiss, 1977:534-535, emphasis added):

Evidence suggests that government officials use research less to arrive at solutions than to orient themselves to problems. They use research to help them think about issues and define the problematics of a situation, to gain new ideas and new perspectives. They use research to help formulate problems and to set the agenda for future policy actions. *And much of this use is not deliberate, direct, and targeted, but a result of long-term percolation of social science concepts, theories, and findings into the climate of informed opinion.* . . .

This kind of diffuse, undirected seepage of social research into the policy sphere can gradually change the whole focus of debate over policy issues. The process is difficult to document, but it appears likely that social research has helped shift the agenda and change the formulation of issues in a wide array of fields: compensatory education, punishment for alcohol and drug offenses, large-scale public housing, institutionalization of the mentally retarded, welfare reform, prepaid health care, child abuse, job training, court reform, and legislative reapportionment. . . .

It is worth noting that the "long-term percolation of . . . concepts, theories, and findings into the climate of informed opinion" is a major benefit of basic research in all fields, entirely apart from direct practical applications. We should not lose sight of the social value of a continuing, cumulative growth of knowledge and understanding. Without regard for the practical payoffs that may follow, our lives are enriched by new and basic discoveries of unforeseen regularity or patterning.

(4) *The federal government is an indispensable and appropriate source of support for basic research.* Basic research is, in the parlance of economists, a public good. Since free exchange and wide dissemination are conditions of its growth, its benefits must be freely available to all and cannot be controlled by those who conduct or have financed the research. Given this and especially given the necessary time lags and unpredictability of research outcomes, there is no reason to expect that either the private sector or federal agencies charged with other missions will serve as adequate sources of support for basic research. The efficient allocation of resources for public goods in general and for basic research in particular is through public funding.

While there is no doubt that important research will continue to be done by researchers operating without funds or with the limited funds they can obtain from their own institutions and from nonfederal sources, a large fraction, perhaps the bulk, of basic research in the behavioral and social sciences would no longer be possible without financial support at levels beyond what these sources—most of them already under heavy pressure—can make available. Adequate funding for basic research in the behavioral and social sciences cannot be provided by dispersed institutional or market forces. Instead, it must continue to be primarily entrusted, as at present, to government agencies whose specific mission is the implementation of a long-term investment strategy with regard to the maintenance and promotion of basic research as a national resource.

The rationale for funding basic research is quite different from prevailing rationales for funding mission-oriented research. Most of the latter, the committee assumes, will continue to be carried on even in the face of severely restricted budgetary conditions. Since mission-oriented research is designed to meet specific needs or problems, largely on an ad hoc basis, funding for it is provided by numerous government agencies, institutions, and private firms as a necessary adjunct to their own ongoing programs. Such a funding pattern by itself, however, makes no provision for continuing replenishment of the stock of insights, ideas, and conceptual as well as analytic tools that grow from the findings of basic research.

Implicit in the foregoing remarks is the assumption that basic research in the behavioral and social sciences must be understood as part of a broader continuum of research activities. Diverse in themselves, the behavioral and social sciences include some disciplines that at their margins merge almost imperceptibly with some of the physical and biological sciences, and others that similarly approach the humanities. Supplementing these continuities in subject matter that cross formal, disciplinary frontiers are similarities in method and outlook that extend across all fields of science. The special complexities, uncertainties, and entanglements of the human subject matter notwithstanding, the behavioral and social sciences are sciences like all others. Hence the same arguments that lead to a judgment to invest public funds in scientific research in general are equally valid for the behavioral and social sciences.

ADDITIONAL CONCLUSIONS

(5) The committee is convinced that the maintenance of some degree of balance among scientific disciplines is in the national interest and that this consideration should enter substantially into the processes of decision making about resources. Estimates of future significance and expectations of practical payoffs are quite possibly as speculative between major scientific domains as they are between alternative research opportunities within a single discipline. Concentrating resources only in selected fields would therefore introduce an unacceptable risk of failing to develop whole sectors of research, the significance of whose findings can be appraised only with considerable uncertainty until long after they are first reported. We wish to point out, however, that an important argument for differential federal support would favor precisely those fields in which the immediate payoffs are least obvious. Where payoffs are obvious, other sources of support generally can be expected. In that sense there may well be a particularly urgent case for the kind of long-term investment strategy that only the federal government can sustain in those fields of inquiry undergoing normal growth but not obviously on the verge of important, publicly recognized breakthroughs that can attract other forms of support.

(6) Irrespective of the gross level of national resources devoted to the support of basic research in the behavioral and social sciences, the committee believes that certain policies for the expenditure of these resources are clearly superior to others. The preeminent principle is the maintenance of continuity insofar as possible. Large, abrupt changes in funding levels, either by

discipline or by problem area, interfere with the orderly planning of research strategies and sharply reduce the effectiveness of whatever funds are available. This is not an argument against making any alteration, but instead for implementating changes slowly and consistently over a period of years. Sudden moves leave little opportunity for consultation, mutual readjustment, and consequent fine-tuning of the relationship between federal agencies and those immediately affected by the introduction of new policies.

A second guiding principle involves the advisability of permanently maintaining a mix or balance among activities receiving research support, even if budgetary pressures become much more serious than we can now foresee. We believe it would be a serious mistake, for example, to accommodate to increasing uncertainties by entirely foreclosing projects that presuppose long-term funding and from which quick payoffs cannot be expected. Longitudinal studies of this kind often offer insights of great potential significance both for basic knowledge and for policy purposes, and they are difficult or impossible to resume once they have been discontinued. Exactly similar arguments apply to the maintenance of large-scale national data banks and research facilities. Ambitious interdisciplinary undertakings are another case in point. Their potential payoff in many unexpected directions is large, even though it may well be accompanied by an increased risk of failure. In other words, to meet budgetary stringencies by concentrating resources on short-term or small-scale or low-risk undertakings would be a prescription not for the survival of the behavioral and social sciences but for the piecemeal destruction of their promise and quality. At the same time, we would not be prepared to argue that short-term or small-scale or low-risk undertakings should be disproportionately sacrificed either. All of these modes of research, singly and in combination, have contributed to the advance of the behavioral and social sciences, and there is no basis for singling out particular modes as most worthy of federal support.

A third guiding principle, pertaining particularly to the social sciences, is that research on foreign cultures should not be cut back disproportionately as a way of coping with budgetary stringencies. Entire disciplines, and substantial parts of others, depend on international research opportunities: anthropology, archaeology, history, comparative politics, development economics, to name only a few. And still other social science disciplines would be well served to expand, rather than contract, their comparative focus. Perhaps because the United States has been the major locus of advancement in most areas of the social and behavioral sciences, much of our knowledge about the structure and functioning of social systems is relatively parochial, restricted far too much to analysis of the United States. Both to understand social patterning in general and to provide a comparative basis for assessing the uniqueness of social arrangements in our own society, social scientists need to be able to do research in many different societies.

(7) A major danger facing the behavioral and social sciences as a result of currently declining support of research is the deflection of talented people into other fields and professions. This threat is exacerbated by simultaneous contraction of opportunities for academic employment, but the latter is a general condition, while the decline of research funding has been relatively more severe in the behavioral and social sciences than in other fields. As already noted, the problem is in one sense likely to be less critical in mission-oriented agencies than in agencies that support basic research, since the decline in their funding will probably be less precipitous. However, we have also taken note previously of the close, synergistic relationship between basic and mission-oriented research, and in particular of the importance to the latter of the continuing enhancement of the stock of new findings and methods derived from basic research. In a deeper sense, therefore, basic and mission-oriented research share the same problem of professional training.

A further consideration makes this problem still more urgent. It is becoming steadily more important not merely to maintain pools of talent at present levels of training and capability but to improve the quality of those pools in order to move in new, and especially interdisciplinary, directions. Among the papers commissioned by the committee, for example, are ones arguing persuasively for a convergence of currently semiautonomous lines of investigation around a new and promising life-course perspective, which may well become a new discipline of its own (Featherman); outlining progress in an area of marked overlap with the physical as well as biological sciences (Braida et al.); and illustrating important complementarities between medicine and the behavioral sciences (Krantz et al.; Wilson). These and others point to a growing need for individual researchers with broadened and enhanced capabilities, even if the total number of researchers is gradually reduced as a result of declining employment and research funding levels. The committee suggests, therefore, that serious attention be given to programs that will increase opportunities for advanced, probably postdoctoral, training.

SUMMARY

The essential themes developed in this report can be briefly summarized. Basic research is carried on in order to create and husband a stock of knowledge, with the confidence that such a stock will be drawn on—for further advances in knowledge as well as for diverse and important practical ends—in ways that seldom can be accurately foreseen. Familiarization with and participation in basic social and behavioral research also play a vital part in graduate professional training. Such training is needed to assess the relevance of available or prospective findings for the design, implementation, and evaluation of social programs. Hence even mission-oriented researchers need to be thoroughly acquainted with the methods and the results of basic research. Neither the creation of new knowledge nor the training of practitioners is an objective that can be most profitably pursued in irregular spurts and pauses or only in relation to narrowly targeted applications. The power of basic research to improve and enrich our lives grows out of the mutual reinforcement and synergism of many interlocking ideas, findings, and practical outcomes. It cannot be understood and properly utilized if we concentrate instead on isolated, product-centered outcomes.

These observations do not provide a prescription for what the sources and level of support of basic research in the behavioral and social sciences should be. But they do suggest that a disinterested, long-term program of support, carried out as a broad, farsighted investment policy rather than to meet the immediate policy objectives of particular agencies, is in the national interest.

References

Altmann, I
   1980   Baboon Mothers and Infants. Cambridge, Mass.: Harvard University Press.
Anastasi, A.
   1976   Psychological Testing. Fourth edition. New York: Macmillan.
Anderson, J. A.
   1980   Cognitive Psychology and Its Implications. San Francisco: W. H. Freeman.
Arrow, K. J.
   1963   Social Choice and Individual Values. Second edition. New York: John Wiley.
Ayllon, T., and N. Azrin
   1968   The Token Economy: A Motivational System for Therapy and Rehabilitation. New York: Appleton-Century-Crofts.
Barton, J.
   1975   Peasants and Strangers: Italians, Rumanians, and Slovaks in an American City, 1890-1950. Cambridge, Mass.: Harvard University Press.
Becker, M. H.
   1979   "Understanding patient compliance: the contributions of attitudes and other psychological factors." In S. J. Cohen, ed., New Directions in Patient Compliance. Lexington, Mass.: D. C. Heath.
Belmont, J. M., and E. C. Butterfield
   1971   "Learning strategies as determinants of mental deficiencies." Cognitive Psychology 2:411-420.
Bender, B.
   1975   Farming in Prehistory: From Hunter-Gatherer to Food Producer. New York: St. Martin's Press.
Bensman, J., and I. Gerver
   1963   "Crime and punishment in a factory: the function of deviancy in maintaining the social system." American Sociological Review 28:588-598.

Bielby, W.
  1981   "Models of status attainment." Pp. 3-26 in D. J. Treiman and R. V. Robinson,
          eds., Research in Social Stratification and Mobility: A Research Annual. Volume
          1. Greenwich, Conn: JAI Press.
Bielby, W., and R. M. Hauser
  1977   "Structural equation models." Annual Review of Sociology 3:137-162.
Binet, A., and T. Simon
  1908   "Le developpement de l'intelligence chez les enfants." L'Annee Psychologique
          14:1-90.
Blau, P. M., and O. D. Duncan
  1967   The American Occupational Structure. New York: John Wiley. Reprinted by
          Free Press.
Bloom, B. S.
  1964   Stability and Change in Human Characteristics. New York: John Wiley.
Brass, W., A. J. Coale, P. Demeny, D. F. Heisel, F. Lorimer, A. Romaniuk, and E. van
de Walle
  1968   The Demography of Tropical Africa. Princeton, N.J.: Princeton University
          Press.
Brown, B., and E. H. Grotberg
  1980   "Head Start: a successful experiment." Courrier 30:337-344.
Buros, O. K., ed.
  1972   The Seventh Mental Measurements Yearbook. Highland Park, N. J.: Gryphon
          Press.
Chase, W. G., D. R. Lyon, and D. A. Ericcson
  1981   "Individual differences in memory span." In M. P. Friedman, J. P. Das, and
          N. O'Connor, eds., Intelligence and Learning. NATO Conference on Intelligence
          and Learning. NATO Conference Series 3, Human Factors: Volume 14. New
          York: Plenum Press.
Chi, M. T. H.
  1976   "Short-term memory limitations in children: capacity or processing deficits."
          Memory and Cognition 4:559-572.
Cole, R. E.
  1980   "Learning from the Japanese: prospects and pitfalls." Management Review
          69:22-42.
Coleman, J. S., E. Katz, and H. Menzel
  1966   Medical Innovation: A Diffusion Study. Indianapolis, Ind.: Bobbs-Merrill.
Coltheart, M., K. Patterson, and J. C. Marshall
  1980   Deep Dyslexia. London: Routledge & Kegan Paul.
Comroe, J. H., Jr., and R. D. Dripps
  1977   The Top Ten Clinical Advances in Cardiovascular-Pulmonary Medicine and
          Surgery, 1945-1975. DHEW (NIH) Publication No. 78-1521. Washington,
          D.C.: U.S. Government Printing Office.
Cox, T.
  1978   Stress. Baltimore: University Park Press.
Cronbach, L. J.
  1970   Essentials of Psychological Testing. Third edition. New York: Harper and Row.
Deming, W. E.
  1968   "Sample surveys: the field." Pp. 13.598-13.612 in D. L. Sills, ed., Encyclopedia
          of the Social Sciences. New York: Macmillan and Free Press.

Donchin, E., W. Ritter, and W. C. McCallum
   1978   "Cognitive psychophysiology: the endogenous components of the ERP." In E. Callaway, P. Tueting, and S. H. Koslow, eds., Event Related Brain Potentials in Man. New York: Academic Press.
Duncan, O. D.
   1961   "A socioeconomic index for all occupations." Pp. 109-138 in Albert J. Reiss, Jr., Occupations and Social Status. New York: Free Press.
Duncan, O. D., D. L. Featherman, and B. Duncan
   1972   Socioeconomic Background and Achievement. New York: Seminar.
Ellins, S. R., S. M. Catalano, and S. A. Schechinger
   1977   "Conditioned taste aversion: a field application to coyote predation on sheep." Behavioral Biology 20:91-95.
The Encyclopaedia Britannica: A Dictionary of Arts, Sciences, The Literature and General Information
   1911   Eleventh edition. Cambridge, England: Cambridge University Press.
Encyclopaedia Britannica: A New Survey of General Knowledge
   1929   Fourteenth edition. London: The Encyclopaedia Britannica Co.
The New Encyclopaedia Britannica
   1974   Fifteenth edition. Chicago: University of Chicago Press.
Erikson, E. H.
   1950   Childhood and Society. New York: Norton.
Erikson, K. T.
   1976   Everything in Its Path: Destruction of Community in Buffalo Creek Flood. New York: Simon and Schuster.
Farley, R.
   1977   "Trends in racial inequalities: have the gains of the 1960s disappeared in the 1970s?" American Sociological Review 42:189-208.
Featherman, D. L.
   1981   "Social stratification and mobility: two decades of cumulative social science." American Behavioral Scientist 24:364-385.
Featherman, D. L., and R. M. Hauser
   1978   Opportunity and Change. New York: Academic Press.
Feldman, H. W., M. H. Agar, and G. M. Beschner, eds.
   1979   Angel Dust: An Ethnographic Study of PCP Users. Lexington, Mass.: Lexington Books.
Field, C. G.
   1980   "Social testing for United States housing policy: the experimental housing allowance program." Pp. 235-282 in Organisation for Economic Co-operation and Development, The Utilization of the Social Sciences in Policy Making in the United States: Case Studies. Paris: Organisation for Economic Co-operation and Development.
Fischer, C. S.
   1976   The Urban Experience. New York: Harcourt Brace Jovanovich.
Fisher, I.
   1922   The Making of Index Numbers: A Study of Their Varieties, Tests, and Reliability. Boston: Houghton Mifflin.
Flannery, K. V.
   1973   "The origins of agriculture." Annual Review of Anthropology 2:271-310.

Geertz, C.
   1980   "Blurred genres—the refiguration of social thought." American Scholar 49:165-179.
Gilbert, J. P., B. McPeek, and F. Mosteller
   1977   "Progress in surgery and anesthesia: benefits and risks of innovative therapy." Pp. 124-169 in J. P. Bunker, B. A. Barnes, and F. Mosteller, eds., Costs, Risks, and Benefits of Surgery. New York: Oxford University Press.
Ginzberg, E., and G. J. Vojta
   1981   "The service sector of the U.S. economy." Scientific American 244:48-55.
Glander, K.
   1977   "Poison in a monkey's Garden of Eden." Natural History Magazine 86:34-41.
Goodman, M., and R. Tashian, eds.
   1976   Molecular Anthropology. New York: Plenum Press.
Gould, L., A. L. Walker, L. E. Crane, and C. W. Lidz
   1974   Connections: Notes from the Heroin World. New Haven, Conn.: Yale University Press.
Grevern, P. J., Jr.
   1970   Four Generations: Population, Land, and Family in Colonial Andover, Massachusetts. Ithaca, N.Y.: Cornell University Press.
Gustavson, C. R., J. Garcia, W. G. Hankins, and K. W. Rusiniak
   1974   "Coyote predation control by aversive conditioning." Science 184(3 May): 581-583.
Gustavson, C. R., D. J. Kelley, M. Sweeney, and J. Garcia
   1976   "Prey-lithium aversions. Part I: Coyotes and wolves." Behavioral Biology 17:61-72.
Hamburg, D. A., and E. R. McCown, eds.
   1979   The Great Apes. Menlo Park, Calif.: Benjamin Cummings.
Hansen, M. H., W. N. Hurwitz, and W. G. Madow
   1953   Sample Survey Methods and Theory. Volumes 1 and 2. New York: John Wiley.
Hareven, T.
   1975   "Family time and industrial time: family and work in a planned corporation town, 1900-1924." Journal of Urban History 1:365-89.
Harlow, H. F., and M. K. Harlow
   1962   "Social deprivation in monkeys." Scientific American 207:136-146.
   1965   "The affectional systems." Pp. 287-334 in A. M. Schrier, H. F. Harlow, and F. Stollnitz, eds., Behavior in Nonhuman Primates. Volume 2. New York: Academic Press.
Hauser, P. M.
   1975   Social Statistics in Use. New York: Russell Sage Foundation.
Heclo, H., and M. Rein
   1980   "Social science and negative income taxation." Pp. 29-66 in Organisation for Economic Co-operation and Development, The Utilization of the Social Sciences in Policy Making in the United States: Case Studies. Paris: Organisation for Economic Co-operation and Development.
Hershberg, T., ed.
   1981   Philadelphia: Work, Space, Family and Group Experience in the 19th Century. New York: Oxford University Press.
Hill, K., H. Zlotnik, and J. Trussell
   1981   Indirect Techniques for Demographic Estimation. Committee on Population and

Demography, National Research Council. Washington, D.C.: National Academy Press.

Hirsch, S. E.
1978   Roots of the American Working Class: Industrialization of the Crafts in Newark, 1800-1860. Philadelphia: University of Pennsylvania Press.

Hochschild, A.
1973   The Unexpected Community. Englewood Cliffs, N.J.: Prentice-Hall.

Hughes, P.
1977   Behind the Wall of Respect: Community Experiments in Heroin Addiction Control. Chicago: University of Chicago Press.

Hunt, J. McV.
1961   Intelligence and Experience. New York: Ronald Press.

Hyman, H., and P. Sheatsley
1964   "Attitudes toward desegregation." Scientific American 211:2-9.

Isaac, G., and E. F. Leakey, eds.
1979   Human Ancestors. San Francisco: W. H. Freeman.

Jencks, C., M. Smith, H. Acland, M. J. Bane, D. Cohen, H. Gintis, B. Heyns, and S. Michelson
1972   Inequality: A Reassessment of the Effect of Family and Schooling in America. New York: Basic Books.

Jencks, C., S. Bartlett, M. Corcoran, J. Crouse, D. Eaglesfield, G. Jackson, K. McClelland, P. Mueser, M. Olneck, J. Schwartz, S. Ward, and J. Williams
1979   Who Gets Ahead? The Determinants of Economic Success in America. New York: Basic Books.

Kandel, D. B.
1980   "Drug and drinking behavior among youth." Pp. 235-285 in A. Inkeles, N. J. Smelser, and R. H. Turner, eds., Annual Review of Sociology. Volume 6. Palo Alto, Calif.: Annual Reviews Inc.

Katz, E., and P. F. Lazarsfeld
1955   Personal Influence. Glencoe, Ill.: Free Press.

Kershaw, D., and J. Fair
1976-   The New Jersey Income-Maintenance Experiment. Three volumes. New York:
1977   Academic Press.

Keyfitz, N.
1968   "Government statistics." Pp. 6.230-6.240 in D. L. Sills, ed., International Encyclopedia of the Social Sciences. New York: Macmillan and Free Press.

Keynes, J. M.
1936   The General Theory of Employment, Interest and Money. London: Macmillan.

Kiesler, S. B., and C. F. Turner, eds.
1977   Fundamental Research and the Process of Education. Final Report to the National Institute of Education by the Committee on Fundamental Research Relevant to Education, National Research Council. Washington, D.C.: National Institute of Education.

Killian, L. M.
1952   "The significance of multiple-group members in disaster." American Journal of Sociology 42:309-314.

Kimble, G.
1968   "Learning: introduction." Pp. 9.114-9.126 in D. L. Sills, ed., International Encyclopedia of the Social Sciences. New York: Macmillan and Free Press.

Kimura, M.
   1979   "The neutral theory of human evolution." Scientific American 241:98-126.
Kleiman, G.
   1975   "Speech recoding in reading." Journal of Verbal Learning and Verbal Behavior
           14:323-329.
Klein, L. R.
   1980   Statement prepared for the National Science Foundation Authorization Hearings,
           Committee on Science and Technology, U.S. House of Representatives, March
           12.
Klineberg, O.
   1935   Negro Intelligence and Selective Migration. New York: Columbia University
           Press.
Koning, H.
   1981   "Onward and upward with the arts [the 11th edition of the Encyclopaedia
           Britannica]." New Yorker 57(March 2):67-68 + .
Kraft, C. L.
   1978   "A psychophysical contribution to air safety: simulator studies of visual illusions
           in night visual approaches." Pp. 363-386 in H. L. Pick, Jr., H. W. Leibowitz,
           J. E. Singer, A. Steinschneider, and H. W. Stevenson, eds., Psychology: From
           Research to Practice. New York: Plenum Press.
Kravis, I. B., Z. Kenessey, A. Heston, and R. Summers
   1975   A System of International Comparisons of Gross Product and Purchasing Power.
           United Nations International Comparison Project, Phase 1. Produced by the
           Statistical Office of the United Nations, the World Bank, and the International
           Comparison Unit of the University of Pennsylvania. Baltimore and London:
           Johns Hopkins University Press.
Kurland, J. A.
   1977   "Kin selection in the Japanese monkey." Contributions to Primatology 12:1-
           145.
Kuznets, S. S.
   1941   National Income and Its Composition: 1919-1938. Two volumes. Publication
           No. 40. New York: National Bureau of Economic Research.
Kuznets, S., and D. S. Thomas,
   1957-   Population Redistribution and Economic Growth, United States, 1870-1950.
   1964   Three volumes. Philadelphia: American Philosophical Society.
Lane, J. P., and J. N. Morgan
   1975   "Patterns of change in economic status and family structure." Pp. 3-60 in G.
           J. Duncan and J. N. Morgan, eds., Five Thousand American Families: Patterns
           of Economic Progress. Volume 3. Analyses of the First Six Years of the Panel
           Study of Income Dynamics. Ann Arbor: University of Michigan, Institute for
           Social Research, Survey Research Center.
Lapham, R. J.
   1978   "Study project, Assembly of Behavioral and Social Sciences: population and
           demography." Pp. 45-54 in The National Research Council in 1978. Washing-
           ton, D.C.: National Academy of Sciences.
Laslett, P.
   1965   The World We Have Lost. London: Methuen.
   1969   "Size and structure of the household in England over three centures." Population
           Studies 23:199-223.

Lazarsfeld, P., B. Berelson, and H. Gaudet
1944   The People's Choice. New York: Duell, Sloan and Pearce.

Leontief, W.
1941   The Structure of the American Economy, 1919-1939: An Empirical Application of Equilibrium Analysis. New York: Oxford University Press.

Levi, L.
1979   "Psychosocial factors in preventive medicine." In Healthy People: The Surgeon General's Report on Health Promotion and Disease Prevention. Background Papers. U.S. Department of Health, Education, and Welfare. DHEW (PHS) Publication No. 79-55071A. Washington, D.C.: U.S. Government Printing Office.

Liebow, E.
1967   Tally's Corner. Boston: Little, Brown.

Loftus, E. F.
1975   "Leading questions and the eyewitness report." Cognitive Psychology 7:560-572.

Lovejoy, C. O.
1981   "The origin of man." Science 211(23 January):341-350.

Lowenstein, J. M.
1980   "Species-specific proteins in fossils." Naturwissenschaften 67:343-346.

Lyon, D. R.
1977   "Individual differences in immediate serial recall: a matter of mnemonics." Cognitive Psychology 9:403-411.

Malthus, Rev. T. R.
1798   An Essay on the Principle of Population, as It Affects the Future Improvement of Society, with Remarks on the Speculations of Mr. Godwin, M. Condorcet, and Other Writers. London: J. Johnson.

Mare, R. D.
1980   "Correlates of achievements." (A review of "Who Gets Ahead? The Determinants of Economic Success in America, by Christopher Jencks and 11 others.") Science 208(16 May): 707-709.

Mason, J. W.
1971   "A re-evaluation of the concept of 'non-specificity' in stress theory." Journal of Psychiatric Research 8:323-333.

Matza, D.
1966   "The disreputable poor." Pp. 310-339 in N. J. Smelser and S. M. Lipset, eds., Social Structure and Mobility in Economic Development. Chicago: Aldine.

Maugh, Thomas H., II
1980   "The 1980 Nobel memorial prize in economics." Science 210(14 November):758-759.

Megaw, J. V. S.
1977   Hunters, Gatherers and First Farmers Beyond Europe. Leicester, England: Leicester University Press.

Mosteller, F.
1981   "Innovation and evaluation." Science 211(27 February):881-886.

Mueller, D. C.
1976   "Public choice: a survey." Journal of Economic Literature 14:395-433.

Myrdal, G.
1944   An American Dilemma: The Negro Problem and Modern Democracy. New York: Harper and Brothers.

National Research Council
  1968   The Behavioral Sciences and the Federal Government (Young report). Washington, D.C.: National Academy of Sciences.
  1976   Social and Behavioral Science Programs in the National Science Foundation: Final Report (Simon report). Washington, D.C.: National Academy of Sciences.
  1978   The Federal Investment in Knowledge of Social Problems. Volume 1. Study Project on Social Research and Development. Washington, D.C.: National Academy of Sciences.
  1981   "The science of cognition." In Outlook for Science and Technology: The Next Five Years. San Francisco: W. H. Freeman.
National Research Council and Social Science Research Council
  1969   The Behavioral and Social Sciences: Outlook and Needs (BASS report). Englewood Cliffs, N.J.: Prentice-Hall.
National Science Board
  1969   Knowledge Into Action: Improving the Nation's Use of the Social Sciences (Brim report). Special Commission on the Social Sciences. Washington, D.C.: National Science Board.
Nelson, T. O., and E. E. Smith
  1972   "Acquisition and forgetting of hierarchically organized information in long-term memory." Journal of Experimental Psychology 95:388-396.
Newell, A., and H. A. Simon
  1972   Human Problem Solving. Englewood Cliffs, N.J.: Prentice-Hall.
Orr, L. L.
  1980   "The health insurance study: expermentation and health financing policy." Pp. 359-376 in Organisation for Economic Co-operation and Development, The Utilization of the Social Sciences in Policy Making in the United States: Case Studies. Paris: Organisation for Economic Co-operation and Development.
Perrow, C.
  1980   Three Mile Island (TMI) and Organizational Research. Unpublished paper. State University of New York at Stony Brook.
Plott, C. R.
  1976   "Axiomatic social choice theory: an overview and interpretation." American Journal of Political Science 20:511-596.
Posner, M. I.
  1978   Chronometric Explorations of Mind. Hillsdale, N.J.: Lawrence Erlbaum Associates.
  1980   "Orienting of attention." Quarterly Journal of Experimental Psychology 32:3-25.
Reed, C. A., ed.
  1977   Origins of Agriculture. The Hague: Mouton Publishers.
Rees, A.
  1968   "Economics." Pp. 4.472-4.485 in D. L. Sills, ed., International Encyclopedia of the Social Sciences. New York: Macmillan and Free Press.
Richard, A. F.
  1981   "Changing assumptions in primate ecology." American Anthropologist 83:517-533.
Roethlisberger, F., and W. J. Dickson
  1947   Management and the Worker. Cambridge, Mass.: Harvard University Press.

Rosenman, R. H., and M. Friedman
1974   "Neurogenic factors in pathogenesis of coronary heart disease." Medical Clinics of North America 58:269-279.
Rosenman, R. H., et al.
1975   "Coronary heart disease in the Western Collaborative Group Study: final follow-up experience of 8 1/2 years." Journal of the American Medical Association 233:872-877.
Rossi, P. H., and K. C. Lyall
1976   Reforming Public Welfare: A Critique of the Negative Income Tax Experiment. New York: Russell Sage Foundation.
Roy, D.
1972   "Efficiency and 'the fix': informal intergroup relations in a piecework machine shop." Pp. 157-172 in J. M. Shepard, ed., Organizational Issues in Industrial Society. Englewood Cliffs, N.J.: Prentice-Hall.
Russell, C. S.
1979   "Applications of public choice theory: an introduction." Pp. 1-25 in C. S. Russell, ed., Collective Decision Making: Applications from Public Choice Theory. Baltimore: Johns Hopkins University Press (published for Resources for the Future).
Sackett, D. L., and R. E. Haynes
1976   Compliance with Therapeutic Regimens. Baltimore: Johns Hopkins University Press.
Savage, L. J.
1954   The Foundations of Statistics. New York: John Wiley.
Schachter, S., et al.
1977   "Studies of the interaction of psychological and pharmacological determinants of smoking." Journal of Experimental Psychology: General 106:3-40.
Schweinhart, L. J., and D. P. Weikart
1980   Young Children Grow Up: The Effects of the Perry Preschool Program on Youths Through Age 15. Monographs of the High/Scope Educational Research Foundation, Number 7. Ypsilanti, Mich.: High/Scope Press.
Selye, H.
1956   The Stress of Life. New York: McGraw-Hill.
Sewell, W. H., and R. M. Hauser
1975   Education, Occupation, and Earnings. New York: Academic Press.
Sherwin, C. W., and R. S. Isenson
1967   "Project Hindsight." Science 156(23 June):1571-1577.
Siegel, P. M.
1971   The American Occupational Prestige Structure. Unpublished Ph.D. dissertation. University of Chicago.
Simon, H. A.
1974   "How big is a chunk?" Science 183(8 February):482-488.
1980   "The behavioral and social sciences." Science 209(4 July):72-78.
1981   "Unity of the arts and sciences: the psychology of thought and discovery." Paper presented at the annual meeting of the American Academy of Arts and Sciences, Boston, May 16.
Smelser, N. J.
1959   Social Change in the Industrial Revolution. Chicago: University of Chicago Press.

Stack, C. B.
1974 All Our Kin: Strategies for Survival in a Black Community. New York: Harper and Row.

Sternberg, S.
1966 "High speed scanning in human memory." Science 153(5 August):652-654.

Stoddard, E. R.
1972 "The informal 'code' of police deviancy: a group approach to 'blue-coat crime.'" Pp. 527-548 in J. M. Shepard, ed., Organizational Issues in Industrial Society. Englewood Cliffs, N.J.: Prentice-Hall.

Stone, L.
1977 The Family, Sex and Marriage in England, 1500-1800. New York: Harper and Row.

Stuart, A.
1968 "Sample surveys: nonprobability sampling." Pp. 13.612-13.616 in D. L. Sills, ed., International Encyclopedia of the Social Sciences. New York: Macmillan and Free Press.

Terman, L. M.
1916 The Measurement of Intelligence. Boston: Houghton Mifflin.

Treiman, D. J.
1977 Occupational Prestige in Comparative Perspective. New York: Academic Press.

Turner, C. F., and E. Martin, eds.
1981 Survey Measurement of Subjective Phenomena: Summary Report. Panel on Survey Measurement of Subjective Phenomena, Committee on National Statistics, National Research Council. Washington, D.C.: National Academy Press.

Tversky, A., and D. Kahneman
1981 "The framing of decisions and the psychology of choice." Science 211(20 January):453-458.

United Nations Department of Economic and Social Affairs
1967 Methods of Estimating Basic Demographic Measures from Incomplete Data. Population Studies No. 2, Manual IV. New York: United Nations.

Van de Geer, J. P.
1971 Introduction to Multivariate Analysis for the Social Sciences. San Francisco: W. H. Freeman.

Washburn, S. L.
1979 "Tools and human evolution." Pp. 9-21 in G. L. Isaac and R. Leakey, eds., Human Ancestors. San Francisco: W. H. Freeman.

Weber, A. F.
1899 The Growth of Cities in the 19th Century: A Study in Statistics. Reprinted 1963. Ithaca, N.Y.: Cornell University Press.

Weiss, C. H.
1977 "Research for policy's sake: the enlightenment function of social science research." Policy Analysis 3:531-545.

Whyte, W. F.
1955 Street Corner Society. Second edition. Chicago: University of Chicago Press.

Wigdor, A. K., and W. R. Garner, eds.
1981 Ability Testing: Uses, Consequences, and Controversies. Report of the Committee on Ability Testing, National Research Council. [Two parts. Part I: Report of the Committee. Part II: Documentation Section.] Washington, D.C.: National Academy Press.

Wirth, L.
    1938   "Urbanism as a way of life." American Journal of Sociology 44:1-24.
Wrangham, R. W.
    1980   "An ecological model of female-bonded primate groups." Behavior 75:262-299.
Wrigley, E. A.
    1969   Population and History. London: Weidenfeld. (Also New York: McGraw-Hill.)
Yerkes, R. M., ed.
    1921   "Psychological examining in the United States army." Memoirs of the National Academy of Sciences XV. Washington, D.C.: U.S. Government Printing Office.
Zorbaugh, H. W.
    1929   The Gold Coast and the Slum. Chicago: University of Chicago Press.

Appendix A
Contents of Part II

*Behavioral and Social Science Research:
A National Resource—Part II* is available from the National
Academy Press.

RESEARCH IN FORMAL DEMOGRAPHY
Jane Menken and James Trussell

THE STUDY OF VOTING
Philip E. Converse, Heinz Eulau, and Warren E. Miller

BEHAVIOR AND HEALTH*
David S. Krantz, David C. Glass, Richard Contrada, and Neal E. Miller

EARNINGS AND THE DISTRIBUTION OF INCOME: INSIGHTS FROM
ECONOMIC RESEARCH
James J. Heckman and Robert T. Michael

CULTURAL MEANING SYSTEMS
Roy G. D'Andrade

THE LIFE-SPAN PERSPECTIVE IN SOCIAL SCIENCE RESEARCH*
David L. Featherman

ADVANCES IN METHODS FOR LARGE-SCALE SURVEYS AND
EXPERIMENTS*
Judith M. Tanur

*Papers prepared jointly for the Social Science Research Council and the Committee on Basic
Research in the Behavioral and Social Sciences.

RESEARCH IN PSYCHOPHYSICS
    L. D. Braida, Tom N. Cornsweet, N. I. Durlach, David M. Green, Alvin
    Liberman, Herschel Leibowitz, R. Duncan Luce, Richard Pew, and Carl
    Sherrick

COGNITIVE DEVELOPMENT IN THE FIRST YEARS OF LIFE
    Katherine Nelson

TERRITORY, PROPERTY, AND TENURE
    Robert M. Netting

READING AS A COGNITIVE PROCESS
    Patricia A. Carpenter and Marcel A. Just

FROM EXPERIMENTAL RESEARCH TO CLINICAL PRACTICE: BEHAVIOR
THERAPY AS A CASE STUDY
    G. Terence Wilson

Appendix B
Biographical Sketches
of Committee Members
and Staff

ROBERT MCC. ADAMS is Harold H. Swift distinguished service professor of anthropology and director of the Oriental Institute, University of Chicago. Previously he also served as director of the Oriental Institute 1962-1968 and as dean of the Division of Social Sciences 1970-1974 and 1979-1980. His archaeological field studies in Iraq, Iran, Syria, Saudi Arabia, and Mexico have primarily concerned the history of land use and urban settlement. He is author of *Land Behind Baghdad* (1965), *The Evolution of Urban Society* (1966), and *Heartland of Cities* (1981) and coauthor of *The Uruk Countryside* (1972). He is a member of the National Academy of Sciences and the American Philosophical Society and a fellow of the American Academy of Arts and Sciences, the American Anthropological Association, and the Middle East Studies Association. He received PhB, AM, and PhD degrees from the University of Chicago.

DAVID A. HAMBURG is director of the Division of Health Policy Research and Education, Harvard University. Previously he was president of the Institute of Medicine 1975-1980, professor and chairman of the Department of Psychiatry at Stanford Medical School 1961-1972, and Sherman Fairchild distinguished scholar at the California Institute of Technology 1974-1975. His research is concerned with psychological stress and endocrine function, psychotherapy in crisis, and genetics, hormones, and behavior. He is coauthor of *The Great Apes* (1979), *Biobehavioral Aspects of Aggression* (1981), and *Health and Behavior: Frontiers of Research in Biobehavioral Sciences* (1982). He is a member of the board of directors of the American Association

117

for the Advancement of Science, a member of the council of the American Academy of Arts and Sciences, past president of the Academy for Behavioral Medicine Research and the International Society for Research on Aggression, and a member and past chairman of the Psychiatric Research Society. He received an MD from Indiana University.

JUANITA M. KREPS, an economist, was U.S. Secretary of Commerce 1977-1981. Previously she was James B. Duke professor of economics at Duke University 1972-1977 and vice president of Duke University 1973-1977. Her research in economics has been in the field of labor economics with special emphasis on retirement and income problems of the elderly. She is author of *Sex and the Marketplace: American Women at Work* (1971) and coauthor of *Principles of Economics* (revised edition 1965) and *Contemporary Labor Economics* (1974). She is a member of the boards of directors of American Telephone and Telegraph, Citicorp, Armco, R. J. Reynolds, J. C. Penney, Eastman Kodak, and UAL Incorporated and a trustee of the Duke Endowment. She received an AB degree from Berea College and MA and PhD degrees from Duke University.

GARDNER LINDZEY, a psychologist, is director of the Center for Advanced Study in the Behavioral Sciences, Palo Alto, California. Previously he held faculty positions at Pennsylvania State University, Western Reserve University, Harvard University, Syracuse University, the University of Minnesota, and the University of Texas. His research involves studies of personality, social psychology, and genetics and behavior. He is coauthor of *Theories of Personality* (1957, 1970, 1978), *Projective Techniques and Cross-Cultural Research* (1961), and *Race Differences in Intelligence* (1975) and editor of the *Handbook of Social Psychology* (1954). He is a member of the Institute of Medicine, the American Academy of Arts and Sciences, and the American Philosophical Society and past president of the American Psychological Association and the Society for the Study of Social Biology. He received AB and MS degrees from Pennsylvania State University and a PhD from Harvard University.

ELIZABETH F. LOFTUS is professor of psychology at the University of Washington. Previously she was on the faculty of the New School for Social Research. Her work in experimental psychology has been in the areas of human memory and eyewitness testimony. She is author of *Eyewitness Testimony* (1979) and *Memory* (1980) and coauthor of *Psychology* (1981) and *Essence of Statistics* (1982). She received a BA from the University of California, Los Angeles, and MA and PhD degrees from Stanford University.

JAMES G. MARCH is Fred H. Merrill professor of management in the Graduate School of Business, Stanford University, and senior fellow at the Hoover Institution. He also holds appointments in political science, sociology, and education at Stanford University. His research is concerned with organizations, decisions, and leadership. He is coauthor of *Organizations* (1958), *A Behavioral Theory of the Firm* (1963), and *Leadership and Ambiguity* (1974). He is a member of the National Academy of Sciences, the National Academy of Education, and the American Academy of Arts and Sciences. He was a member of the National Science Board 1968-1974 and of the National Council of Educational Research 1974-1978. He received a BA from the University of Wisconsin and MA and PhD degrees from Yale University.

JESSICA T. MATHEWS is a member of the editorial board of *The Washington Post*. Previously she was director of the office of global issues of the National Security Council 1977-1979, director of issues and research for the 1976 presidential campaign of Morris Udall, and a congressional science fellow of the American Association for the Advancement of Science 1973-1974. Her research interests in biophysics and biochemistry have focused on molecular mechanisms and the control of development. She has been a member of the Committee on Scientific Freedom and Responsibility and the Committee on Science and Public Policy of the American Association for the Advancement of Science. She received a BA from Radcliffe College and a PhD from the California Institute of Technology.

PHILIP MORRISON is Institute professor of physics at the Massachusetts Institute of Technology. His research focuses on the application of principles of physics to astronomy. He is the author of many research papers in high-energy astrophysics and since 1964 has been a book reviewer for *Scientific American*. He is a member of the National Academy of Sciences and the International Astronomical Union, a fellow of the American Physical Society, and a founding member and former chairman of the Federation of American Scientists. He received a BS from Carnegie Institute of Technology and a PhD from the University of California, Berkeley.

CHARLES A. MOSHER was a member of the U.S. House of Representatives from the 13th district of Ohio 1961-1977. He was also adjunct professor in science policy of the George Washington University, acting executive director of the House Committee on Science and Technology 1977-1978, and a fellow at the Woodrow Wilson International Center for Scholars 1980-1981. His career has also included positions as editor-publisher of community newspapers. He is a trustee of Oberlin College. He received an AB degree from Oberlin College.

KENNETH PREWITT, a political scientist, is president of the Social Science Research Council. Previously he was director of the National Opinion Research Center and professor of political science at the University of Chicago. His research interests include the recruitment of political leaders and issues affecting national science policy. He is author of *The Recruitment of Political Leadership* (1970) and *Labyrinths of Democracy* (1973). He is a member of the American Academy of Arts and Sciences. He received a BA from Southern Methodist University, an MA from the University of Washington, and a PhD from Stanford University.

PAUL A. SAMUELSON is Institute professor of economics at the Massachusetts Institute of Technology. His research focuses on economic analysis and policy formation, for which he won the Nobel memorial award in economics in 1970. He is author of *Foundations of Economic Analysis* (1947), *Linear Programming and Economic Analysis* (1958), and *Collected Scientific Papers* (Volumes 1 and 2, 1966; Volume 3, 1972; Volume 4, 1977). He is a member of the National Academy of Sciences, the American Philosophical Society, and the American Academy of Arts and Sciences. He is past president of the Econometric Society, the American Economic Association, and the International Economics Association. He received a BA from the University of Chicago and MA and PhD degrees from Harvard University.

NEIL J. SMELSER is University professor of sociology at the University of California, Berkeley. His work involves the sociology of economic development and economic institutions, social change, and collective behavior and social movements. He is author of *Social Change in the Industrial Revolution* (1959) and *Theory of Collective Behavior* (1963). He is a member of the American Philosophical Association and the American Academy of Arts and Sciences. He received a BA degree from Harvard College, BA and MA degrees from Oxford University, and a PhD from Harvard University, and he completed training in psychoanalysis at the San Francisco Psychoanalytic Institute.

SAM BASS WARNER, JR., is William Edwards Huntington professor of history and social science at Boston University. His professional interests center on the history of cities. He is author of *Streetcar Suburbs, The Process of Growth in Boston 1870-1900* (1962), *The Private City, Philadelphia in Three Periods of Its Growth* (1968), *The Urban Wilderness, A History of the American City* (1972), and *The Way We Really Lived, Social Change in Metropolitan Boston Since 1920* (1978). He is a member of the executive council of the Organization of American Historians. He was a member of the advisory council of the United States National Archives 1969-1972. He received AB and PhD degrees from Harvard University.

ROBERT B. ZAJONC is professor of psychology at the University of Michigan and program director of the Research Center for Group Dynamics. His research involves cognitive processes, social facilitation, and family configuration and intelligence. He is author of *Social Psychology* (1965) and *Animal Social Behavior* (1972). He is a member of the American Academy of Arts and Sciences. He received BA, MA, and PhD degrees from the University of Michigan.

DONALD J. TREIMAN is professor of sociology at the University of California, Los Angeles, from which he took a leave of absence to serve as study director of the committee. His work is in the fields of social stratification and mobility, especially cross-national comparisons, and labor force demography. He is author of *Occupational Prestige in Comparative Perspective* (1977). He is a member of the Population Association of America and of the research committee on stratification of the International Sociological Association. He has a BA from Reed College and MA and PhD degrees from the University of Chicago.